TASHENA ANDERSON-PLACE

Fill Your Cup

DISCOVERING THE
WAR BETWEEN
LIFE AND FAITHFULNESS

Photo courtesy of John Macaspac, Macaspac Photography

For all the special times that we've had, and for all the special times I hoped were to come. I dedicate this book to you. The one who believed in everything that I did. The one who knew what was needed not only for our family, but for the community. To the one who was the official game changer, the one we all looked up to, the one who always put God first, the one who would give you her last if you needed it, the one who loved harder than anyone I've ever known.

Her mom, my nanny, his grandmother-in-law, their great-grandmother, your aunt, your cousin, your principal, your teacher, your friend, your Deaconess, and your church clerk, Gladys H. Anderson.

Life will never be the same without you.
Until we meet again. I love you!

Fill Your Cup

In times where isolation and loneliness run rampant despite being the most connected society in history, this book will bring you a dose of intimacy as Tashena bravely peels back the layers of her life. She boldly reveals the reality of life's challenges when we live self-centered and the incredible transformation that can happen when we accept Jesus into our hearts and strive to live Christ-centered instead. I'm honored to have seen the birth of a thought turn into pages of testimony, into a book of incredible truth and encouragement. Perfect for anyone in the mood for a chat over coffee, Tashena masterfully befriends the reader right from the start, and like any good conversation, you'll find it hard to put down! I suggest starting with a cup full of your favorite drink, access to refills, and tissues handy as you dive deep into raw, real-life stories with God's mercy and goodness on display. A cup is just a cup until it is filled.

Jen Yeates

– TABLE OF CONTENTS –

– FOREWORD –

I imagine that you selected this book possibly because of its captivating cover or maybe because you need encouragement, healing, or restoration. Let me be the first to tell you that you have come to the right place. I have witnessed firsthand the constant warfare that my best friend/sister, Tashena Anderson-Place, has faced and overcame with the power of God fighting alongside her.

Throughout these pages, you will embark on a journey with her as she unfolds her story of living through hard, tumultuous times, discovering radical faith and restoration that only God Himself was able to supply her. Do not fret, my friends, God wants to do the same for you if you let Him. God is closer than our very own breath and will breathe life into our circumstances where we can only see hopelessness. This is what He did for Tashena and her family and will do for you.

As you begin to read this book, whatever you are dealing with, whether currently or from your past, my prayer is that you will be reminded of our Heavenly Father's amazing love for you through His Word, which is dispersed throughout every section. It has been an absolute pleasure to witness her infectious and contagious love and faith, which she received from Jesus and spreads to everyone she encounters. The passion and gratitude that Tashena has for and in our Heavenly Father exudes out of her and onto the pages. It is truly an honor and a privilege to call her my best friend/sister, and I am ecstatic to introduce you to her in these words.

Love,

Trameca Clanton

the Defining Moment

CHAPTER ONE

A Cup is Just a Cup

Where Do I Begin?

The pink one? The green one? The one that has the perfect inspirational verse on it or tells me how I am feeling today? The one with sparkles? There are so many choices when it comes to the perfect cup, but what I've found is what's on the outside is not as important as what I pour into the cup.

My goal for this book is not to seem like I have all the answers (believe me, I am still learning) but to share my testimony, my belief, my grief, the mountains, and the valleys in hopes that it will grow your faith, strengthen your spirit, and point you back to our loving Father.

You're probably wondering how I ended up as a Christian author–me too! As many people know, I was not always on this path. I have always believed in a higher power, but boy, did I lose my way. I'll give you a little background, and then we'll get started.

I was born and raised in a small, rural town on the outskirts of Richmond, Virginia. Everyone knows us by the motto "Virginia is for lovers," but we are so much more than that. Virginia was a wonderful place to grow up, but I quickly discovered that I was ambitious and very goal-oriented. I knew there was so much more to see in the world than in my home state. So, I was always looking for the right opportunity to move. I even tried to convince my mom when I started looking for colleges to let me attend Spelman in Georgia and Michigan State–you know that didn't happen. She was not letting her only child, her only daughter, move thousands of miles away. I get it now, but at first, I thought she wanted to smother me.

Growing up, I was raised in a Baptist household. So, as you can imagine, church was taken pretty seriously. My wonderful grandmother was the church clerk, Deaconess, Superintendent of the Sunday School, President of the Missionary Ministry, President of the Senior Choir, Directress of Vacation Bible School, Organizer of the Deaconess Ministry, Sponsor of the Junior Missionary Ministry, Member of the Pastoral Search Committee, and the Church Anniversary, Constitution, and By-Laws Committee. In the community, she participated as an Eastern Star. As you can see, she was the reason I even knew who God was. She served Him wholeheartedly until she couldn't any longer.

I decided to get baptized before I hit my teen years. I'll never forget the day I walked to the front of the church to accept Christ as my Savior. My grandmother was standing there in her Sunday best. In the South, when we say "Sunday best," that means she had on the matching hat, the perfect dress, shoes, and accessories to match. I used to spend time in her room, admiring all her beautiful clothes. She was truly such a lady.

Just as church was important while growing up, so was my education. My grandmother was also a school teacher and eventually principal. As you can see, we take on many duties in a small town. While grading her papers, she would make me sit and read or work on worksheet pages from the upper grades she was teaching. She also loved to sit me at the dining room table with mathematical flashcards. It sounds intense, but it never bothered me. She had a vision for me and knew I could achieve whatever I set my mind to. Her confidence and guidance did rub off–I went on to obtain an Associate's degree (Suma Cum Laude), Bachelor's degree (Magna Cum Laude), and a Master's degree in Business Administration after high school graduation. My family would always joke that I'd be the first one in the family to be a professional student. I can see why they thought that. I often debate getting my Doctorate now but want to focus on what I feel God needs me to do currently, being a wife and mother. For years, success, graduations, and promotions controlled me. All of it came with a price and a persona that was nothing to be proud of, really. It has been very freeing to let go of those thoughts for a bit and see what is really important.

Along this journey, I met my husband, Jayshawn. We were twenty-one years old when we met in 2007. Now, we are headed into our fifteenth year of being together and our twelfth year of marriage. At twenty-one, we were still babies, and I know for me, I had no business being in a committed relationship. I guess I couldn't resist saying hello to a guy from Bermuda. He and I met via MySpace. I would have never guessed that would be my love story. I thought it would be a college love that ended up asking me to marry him at graduation. See, we have our own expectations, but life has a way of going the opposite of what we're thinking. I am thankful that he has stuck in here with me all this time. We've had our days when it wasn't pretty, we've considered divorce, but you know, once you sit back and think about it, the good outweighs the bad. I love the way my pastor describes marriage. He always says, "Marriage is two imperfect people coming together to try and make one life together. What's even harder is when you don't have God in the mix." He hit the nail right on the head. The years before we fully gave our lives over to Christ were much different than our time together now. We always laugh that we wasted so much time being angry with each other. All of it was around communication and expectation. If I can give any advice, it would be to try to communicate openly, don't live in comparison to other relationships, and please have realistic expectations. Jesus is truly the only one who is of man and God without sin or imperfection.

Now that you know a little about my imperfect background and all the cards are on the table, let's begin.

I hope you can see that it won't always be flawless. You will feel like you're confused, constantly in trial or change, but believe me, you have to stay the course. There is something so beautiful at the end of your journey, and you know what?

God brought me right here, to you! Yes, you, and that is exactly where He needs me at this moment, in this season. Remain in Him, stay faithful. There is grace in the waiting.

P.S. I have added note and prayer pages at the end of each chapter in hopes that you will fill them with your own thoughts, hopes, struggles, and victories.

Psalm 40:1-2

"I waited patiently for the Lord to help me and he turned to me and heard my cry. He lifted me out of the pit of despair, out of the mud and the mire. He sat my feet on solid ground and steadied me as I walked along." (NLT)

Notes

Notes

Prayers

_____
_____
_____
_____
_____
_____
_____
_____
_____
_____
_____
_____
_____
_____
_____
_____
_____
_____
_____

– CHAPTER TWO –

Holy Grounds

A Cup of Faith

"Welcome, may I offer you a sample of our newest coffee? We call it Holy Grounds."

When I began diving into writing this book, I started thinking, what if I change my scenery a bit while writing? I believe trying new things can bring about a fresh perspective. Where else can you get the perfect cup of coffee and faith in one place but a Christian coffee shop? After hearing the barista offer this newest coffee, I began thinking about what to call this cup—a cup of Holy, or maybe a cup of Faith—since it takes faith to even realize or believe you are on holy ground.

So, what is faith? I'll have to admit that the answer to this question must be one of the most sought-after. In this context, I can only give you my two cents about what I think it means and how I've seen it defined in hopes that you can connect with it. Faith, in my opinion, is believing, completely trusting, in something or someone. It is strong confidence that this person or entity you believe in has your best interest at heart and that what they say is true. This type of belief seems to resonate with your soul.

I can't say that I always get this right, but I do know that having faith has gotten me through some of the highs and lows in life in ways that I couldn't imagine. At times, having faith feels like having a secret superpower. It affects how we walk, talk, and view our current situations. It can cause your family or closest friends to question, "What's gotten into you?" Maybe you're smiling more or feeling joy when most wouldn't. Maybe you've picked up a giving spirit. It all stems from faith.

Choosing to pick up faith is a constant, minute-by-minute, daily duty. I know there are many times I catch myself throughout my day saying, "Lord, they are going to make me take off my little bit of Jesus." Can you picture that in your mind? I often see it as a coat that I am wearing that I can take off and put right back on. The funny thing about that is we aren't even supposed to take Him off. As I just stated, it's our secret superpower; it will be tested, and how we respond is important.

Faith is a two-way street between you and God the Father, God the Son, and God the Holy Spirit. Faith doesn't have to be automatic. Faith can build. Faith can change. Faith gives hope. This belief has helped me many times especially in the process of reconciliation. An example in my life of hope rebuilding is my relationship with my dad.

Over the last few years, my dad and I have finally found something that he and I can connect on other than cooking. I have to say, God works in mysterious ways. He is the King of restoration. My dad and I still have a ways to go, but we are better than we were. A little back story—my dad left my mom and me when I was ten years old. My parents were very young when they had me, so I guess we can chalk this up to growing pains. When he left, my mom, along with my grandmother, took over raising me. I would visit him occasionally, but I had a very impressionable mind then. Seeing him live with another family did not sit well with me, and my mother knew that. They would argue over me constantly, and my dad thought my mom was controlling what I wanted to do and think, but honestly, it was all wrong. As a child, we are taught the difference between right and wrong early on. I knew enough to know that our world was upside down.

As time passed and I got older, we stopped talking and visiting each other. Sometimes I try to recall what caused this gap in communication, but I can't remember. I was in my twenties when my dad came back into my life. At this point, I was married and trying to build my own family. The one thing that drove me crazy was his need to apologize for the past every time we spoke. I know it sounds bad, but you can never heal if you are always looking backward. He and I didn't really have a relationship, and he didn't know me–well, the older version of me. It felt like he couldn't get past the ten-year-old little girl that he left behind. Finally, one day, I told him that in order for us to continue speaking, he must never cry or bring up the past again. We have to heal forward, or we cannot be in each other's lives. We weren't getting anywhere, and I wanted us to move on. It was a harsh way to explain it to your parent, but at that point, it was needed. Now, we are much better because of it. He thanks me a lot for having that real conversation with him. Sometimes the hardest conversations can birth a new blessing.

When I told my dad I was writing a book, he was elated. He has grown to be one of my greatest cheerleaders. It is great to see how proud he can be. He was even gracious enough to share with me a letter that he wrote during a portion of his life when he felt lost and that his faith had diminished. I felt like it was a great example of repentance. He showed that even when it doesn't seem like anything good could go right in your life, when the walls are closing in, when the negative thoughts are growing, when the grass is looking greener, all we have to do is ask, have faith, and believe, then miracles start happening. It's like a door begins to open for change to start taking place on our behalf. Faith is what gets us through the valley. Faith is what meets us around the mountain. Faith is where grace and glory meet. Faith puts us right at His feet. A place we shouldn't ever want to leave. God is so gracious. We can turn away and return to Him, knowing He will never change. His door will always be open. Faith brings deliverance. Let's take a look...

Dear Lord,

I come to You with the plans I have for my life. I want to live in Your presence. My plan is to be Your servant. Just as Ezra did in the Bible. I will confess my sins to You, Father. I will ask for directions on the best way to restore my relationship with You. True repentance does not end with words of confession—that would be mere lip service.

We must also be led to corrected behavior and changed attitudes. When we sin against Your will, we must ask for forgiveness and be ready to accept Your grace and mercy. Transformation must happen with our thoughts, our words, and our actions. It must be a true recommitment. I will continue to serve and take care of all that You have entrusted me with. I will serve You wholeheartedly.

I have realized that my past has consumed me. The abandonments, no reconciliation, and all of the negative thoughts are strongholds. My pathway at times looks narrow, but my love for You is wide. You said to me that I am nothing without You being the driving force internally and externally. May I lay my life at Your feet? Take me, Father, by the hand, lead me, guide me. I will forever praise and glorify Your holy and everlasting Name.

Your faithful servant, Brian

When I first read this letter, I thought, "Wow, how honest and pure." How amazing that my dad wanted to be taken by the hand, demonstrating childlike faith. Seeing him vulnerable before God was refreshing. It adjusted my heart posture towards God. I had to look back over my relationship to see if I had also freely opened myself to all He had or wanted from me. Had I truly repented or asked God to strengthen my faith? He is almighty, and I believe life is so much better with Him. I have faith in this same belief for you as well.

Have you ever heard anyone say, "If only you have faith as small as a mustard seed?" I remember being in church and someone showing me the size of a mustard seed.

It blew my mind. I was taken aback because Jesus said that all I need to do is have faith the size of this seed that was no bigger than a period on the paper, and I can do anything. It is so amazing what He can do if we let him. The mustard seed could easily be a decision to change something you do not normally do, like waking up and simply saying, "Thank you, Lord, for waking me up this morning," inserting a worship song into your schedule, or reading one line of scripture. All He is asking is for you to be good soil so that the seed within you can grow. Jesus knows what is there. We just have to kick out the rocks, destroy the weeds, feed it with the Word, water it, and be good stewards of it. It may not look like much in the beginning, but those small, gradual changes will eventually turn into the most beautiful blossom connected to the vine of life.

There is the most perfect song that goes along with this truth. It is called "Isaiah Song" by Maverick City Music. Their words remind me of the barren, dry land that we have. There is soil within us that needs to be tended to again. As I am listening, I envision a drop of water falling from the skies to renew all that is there. Have faith, my friends. It is hard, but we can do hard things.

Hebrews 11:1

"Now faith is the assurance of things hoped for, the conviction of things not seen." (ESV)

Ephesians 2:8-9

"For by grace you have been saved through faith. And this is not your own doing; it is the gift of God, not a result of works, so that no one may boast." (ESV)

Matthew 17:20

"Truly I tell you, if you have faith as small as a mustard seed, you can say to this mountain, 'Move from here to there,' and it will move. Nothing will be impossible for you." (NIV)

Notes

Prayers

CHAPTER THREE

Ristretto or Lungo?

Do I Have What it Takes?

"Ristretto or Lungo?" she asks the young man standing in line. I am no coffee connoisseur, and sometimes I resort to the only thing I know that has all the answers, Google. Ristretto and Lungo are shots of espresso. One is considered a short shot and the other a long shot. Of course, after finding my illustrious research answer, I felt like there was something that stuck out to me. In life, we always discuss our short-term and long-term goals, taking the easy route or the long way, immediate or late gratification. We question ourselves about the next promotion or big decision. I believe we call it weighing our pros and cons.

"I can do anything I set my mind to!"
"I'd be great at that...maybe."

"I was born to do this!"
"I'm too old."

"They won't consider me."
"It's a lot of work."

Does that sound familiar?

Over the years, I've learned that I can be my own worst critic. I had high expectations, big goals, and a big ego. Of course, I didn't see that then, but eventually, the inevitable began to happen. I grew up!

When we face challenges in life or feel pushed to try something new, we immediately get nervous, excited, or doubtful. It's like we go through stages of talking ourselves in and out of the situation.

These types of conversations with ourselves are exactly what keep us in limbo unable to make the decision, unable to leap, unable to discern the voice of God. Guess what I call that? I call that being dazed and confused. It's a tactic used in spiritual warfare.

Think about this—when you are faced with a challenging situation, like getting your child to the car, but the biggest bug you've ever seen is blocking the way, you have to think of a plan, right? There is no way you or your child will make it through without it seeing the both of you. So, a parent does what they know best. The dazed and confused tactic! You get the bug spray and spray it just enough to make it weak and vulnerable. It is no longer a threat to you. It is fumbling all around, and now you can take advantage of the situation. Off to the car you go!

This is exactly what the enemy does to us! When we are on this life journey, the enemy sees us as a threat. He wants to get past us by all means necessary through our thoughts, those around us, and most importantly, our beliefs. He will keep spraying us with doubt, hurt, and loss, so that we are vulnerable. He wants to do this to keep you distracted from your true purpose, the gift living inside of you. He is afraid you'll notice who you truly are, your true name, your true Father. He laughs in the shadows, looking for the next moment he can sneak in to make you dazed and confused.

We need to realize that God chose all of us the day Jesus went to the cross. He loved us so much He wanted to do whatever it would take to bring us to Him. Don't let the enemy poke holes in the armor that God has given you. You are everything that God says you are!

- His child
- Made in His image
- Filled with His Spirit
- A mighty warrior

The devil does not waste his time on those he knows would be easy targets. He wants the ones who threaten his agenda. We need to view ourselves through God's eyes—seek Him during the trials, the good times, in our daily lives, and definitely in decision making.

You have what it takes because we have nothing to fear. We should be confident in this. It is okay to wonder, but the point is not to stay stagnant.

Some of the greatest ideas started with just a thought. For example, do you think I knew that I'd be focused on ministry and writing this book? Of course not! Remember, in the beginning, my biggest goal was to be in the C-suite and single.

Go back and look at how many times I said: I was, I thought, or I wanted. It was a lot, right? Those statements are called earthly expectations. We are either taught these ways from childhood or learn them as we grow up. Did you hear me say that I went to God in prayer to ask Him who I am or what my purpose was? No.

That's what we need to do to determine if we have what it takes or if the door we see is for us. If we don't, that is when we end up distracted, confused, heartbroken, right where the enemy wants us. He loves when we put ourselves in our way. It makes it easier for him. We are doing all the work for him, and he is reaping the benefits.

We love viewing different fields of flowers but not tending to the one God has placed before us. We are continuously searching for more when we haven't put in the work or time to see or hear what is needed from us. How do you think comparison works?

Seeing someone else's brightly colored, shiny new blessing is not easy–it brings about comparison. Just that quick, without knowing it, we are walking with "why not me?" syndrome (hint, hint, dazed and confused).

God's timing is different from our timing. It is good to be patient, have grace, and know that the work being put in now will bloom into the breakthrough desired.

- Will it be easy? No.
- Will you be uncomfortable? Most likely.
- Will you be given every answer immediately? Not happening.

That's the beauty of God's love. He wants us to figure out the puzzle. He wants us to seek Him. He wants us to watch His glory unfold. He is magnificent and orchestrates every second and every detail. It blows my mind, and my heart begins to swell thinking about it. All of this is for us, and it is only a glimpse of what's to come when we join Him one day.

God is going to build you up and prepare you for what He is calling you to do. You are going to get weary–stay focused. You are going to question if you are hearing Him correctly–you are. You are going to say, "It can't be me," but it is. You are going to say, "How will I do this?"– just believe. These are the moments we need to lean in closer to Him. Seek counsel with those that you consider or could become spiritual family. Consult a mentor, pray, read the Word, find a podcast, play your favorite playlist (Maverick City Music), and let go of the anxiety.

Just know you have what it takes because GOD SAID SO!

It is written, and it is done. You've been saved. You are His child. ACT LIKE IT!

Yes, it sounds like I'm yelling at you, but it is only because I wish I had known that sooner. I wasted way too many years not in His presence. I was driving the car of life when I should have been the passenger.

I wasted ten years in a daze, not having the marriage and relationship that we have now.

I wasted twenty years ignoring the nudge to be closer to God.

I wasted five years of my son's life being unhappy, in the darkness, tainted by an unforgiving, broken heart.

The best part about all of this...God still loved me and never gave up. He aligned my steps and told me, "It's not too late. I see you, My child." He raised His voice and said, "It's time." I'll never forget it. I jumped out of my sleep, and there was no one there. But I felt an urgency to listen and take action. I told my husband, "I think God is saying today is the day. We must go to church." He looked at me strangely but agreed. I remembered that a friend of mine had recommended a church to me right before we moved. I thought that was weird, but she knew I had been attending online at a church in Virginia that was similar to this one. I went back to find the name of the church on the post and noticed we were just in time for the next service. That day, in 2017, I was the one out of ninety-nine. He reached out His hand for me, and this time...I grabbed a hold of it, and believe me, I am never looking back.

Not because I am worried about what I'll see there, but because He has shown me what it feels like to remain in His glory here.

I want that for you because you are my brothers and sisters in Christ, and you have what it takes! You just have to activate it by faith.

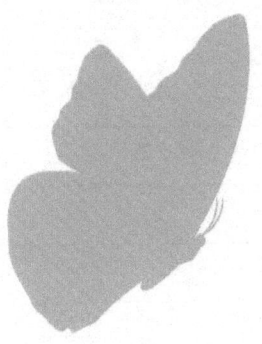

Psalm 138:3

"In the day when I cried out, you answered me and made me bold with strength in my soul." (NKJV)

Notes

Prayers

– CHAPTER FOUR –

to Order or Not to Order?

Doing What I Should Do

"I'll take the next in line. How may I help you today?" The line always seems to move faster when I don't know what I would like from the menu. If I could have it my way, I would have a little bit of everything, but that is never the case. Sometimes I step to the side just to admire the environment and decide if I'm going to order or not. There is always some type of reading or marketing material around that can persuade me to lean one way or the other. In my opinion, the same can be said about our faith, and what I find interesting is that our Father has provided a book that lays out our path, His expectations, His cheat sheet to life, a blueprint, a guiding light. How could the test get any easier?

Throughout life, I've realized that I've always had good intentions to do what I should do and what is expected of me. I finished high school, graduated college multiple times, and created my own little family—picture perfect, it would seem, easy peasy. But even after all the success and happy moments, I still felt lost. Not that I couldn't see the good life I had, but I was constantly drifting. I always needed to move to the next greatest thing to fill the hunger inside to be the best. I had no investment in any of the places, things, or people in my life. If I didn't like it, it was gone. If it got too hard, it was out. If someone addressed me in a way I didn't like, off with their head! Does that sound Christian-like to you? My cup had leaks, and I needed to patch them up.

I can remember feeling untouchable. I carried my head high and was always waiting for someone to challenge my skills or smarts. I always had the next greatest thing lined up. People would ask, "What's next for you, Shena?" I would have a list of things to focus on, and God was not one of them, now not to say that God wasn't present in my life. As I stated earlier in the book, my grandmother ensured I knew God, but just because you bring the horse to water, doesn't mean it will drink.

My life had an idol. I wasn't walking around with a golden calf as they did in the Old Testament, but I did have my back turned to God, going my own way. One thing I know now is that He will allow you to wander from Him because He knows there will be a great lesson that comes from it all. I knew best, I was doing me, and it all felt amazing for a period.

I am laughing now at all this because I truly believed I had it all together. No one knew what I was dealing with but my closest friends during this part of my life. I had my car repossessed twice; I wasn't making the salary that I am now; I sometimes couldn't afford to go out, so I would say I couldn't make it; if I did go out, I was drinking a lot. I've had some not-so-pretty moments with the temple God gave me that I should have reconsidered, but at the time, I thought it was cool. Better yet, most of what I was getting into, I did because my flesh and ego desired it. I could do it, so I did it. No one was there to set any boundaries once I became an adult.

I felt like I set a high standard for myself, and most of it was actually a facade. The only reason that I needed this facade was because I wanted to be known as everything but the small town, Louisa girl. I never wanted to be stuck there. It was a constant joke between people about getting out, and I was not about to be another statistic. When people would ask where I was from, I would say Richmond. They didn't need to know my actual location. It hurts to even write this now because my hometown has always been full of love and wonderful people. I wish I could have kept that in my heart instead of wishing for the high-life.

Holding up my pedestal and crown was hard. The further I pushed myself, the bigger the rooms I had to step in, the larger the facade. I feel like I lost a lot of Tashena during those years. I was looking for confirmation and acceptance from everyone but the One who mattered the most. God didn't care about my resume. He never cared about the house I lived in or the car I drove. He knew where I was going and that, eventually, I would relinquish control. Many of us walk around looking for a sign that it's time to give ourselves back to Christ. I promise He doesn't come down with a red flashing sign saying, "Turn now, here I am," although we sometimes wish He would. God is way smoother than that. He is the one who sends the perfect song, the friend you haven't heard from, or the grandparent trying to give guidance or be the example. He is in everything, all around us.

If I can give you any advice on doing what you should do, I would say to seek Him on your own because the only one that can bring you into a relationship with Him is you. Once you say yes and show that you are a willing vessel, the blessings will overflow. His voice, needs, and purpose will be clear, and you can discern what is from Him and what is not. I am by no means saying that every day will be perfect, but I am saying open your eyes, let go of the old expectations, and pick up the new life that He wants for you.

We SHOULD be able to show God our true selves. He already knows us! What can we hide?

We SHOULD be able to give Him our time—in the car, in the shower, in the morning, in the evening, for five minutes, for twenty minutes, through a worship song or a book. There is no limit to how we can spend time with Him. It doesn't have to be what someone else is doing, be original. Eventually, you will build a routine, and He will bring His presence when you're open and available–don't miss it. His presence could feel like a repeating thought, a passage from the Bible that you remember, a book title you're drawn to (hint, hint, you're in the right place), a song whose words stand out to you, or a video that randomly shows up on social media that relates to your situation. It is not a coincidence; it is meant for you. If it all sounds the same or has a similar message, listen.

I <u>SHOULD</u> be able to trust that God is always working for my good.

I <u>SHOULD</u> be able to be in community with others and share my testimony.

I <u>SHOULD</u> love my brothers and sisters with the grace and mercy He gives us daily.

Sound familiar? Some of this was laid out for us in the commandments given to Moses. See Exodus 20:1-17 or Deuteronomy 6:4-9.

We should listen, study, search, ask, pray, hear, and act like whose we are because He has determined who we are.

John 15:5

"I am the vine; you are the branches.
If you remain in me and I in you,
you will bear much fruit; apart from
me you can do nothing." (NIV)

Notes

Notes

Prayers

Here Comes Jesus

the Slow Pour

I Take Responsibility

As I sit here, listening to all the sounds in the room, one distinct sound catches my attention, the coffee pour. I start to imagine a large coffee cup handed to me and being asked by God to hold it while the coffee is poured slowly. This cup is heavy and the pour is so slow that I can hear the drops first and then must watch the coffee level rise, inch by inch, and how can I say no? The slow pour is exactly how I felt facing the woman in the mirror.

Let's roll back to August 2017. It was our first month in Florida. We uprooted our family in an act of obedience and alignment to what we felt was a blessing from God. I had been offered a lateral transfer opportunity that I knew would eventually lead to other advancement opportunities.

This opportunity meant there would be a fresh start for me, our family, and our marriage. To be honest, my husband and I were not in the best place during this time. I had considered giving up, but it never felt like the right thing to do.

I looked back over my life to consider examples of what to do. My mother and father divorced when I was young. My dad left when I was around the age of ten. My mom made sure to raise me to be strong-willed and independent. Who could blame her, right? She was young and probably thought he was her forever. Since then, she has always had a wall of protection built up around her. To this day, she is very straight to the point and matter of fact when it comes to relationships. I wanted to lean on her, but I knew her advice would not be the middle of the road or compromising. Again, that isn't her fault; it was just the trauma of the past hindering her perspective. The best part, though, is that through the years, my parents have become better with their issues. Are they together? No, but they are cordial.

I was at a crossroads of celebration and bitterness. In my mind, I was choosing between my way of dealing with our issues or following the example I had seen through my parents and other families. My husband and I had agreed that if this move didn't help our situation, we would stay cordial for our son and separate. No one truly wants to see that happen, but sometimes, it can't be avoided.

Let's move forward to October 2017. This was when I heard the calling from God that I spoke of in the last chapter. Here's a closer look at how that morning went.

When we arrived at the church, I sat in the car for a moment because the last time I'd physically been in a church had been years. This was it. He had called me, but was I ready? Do I listen or turn away? I still have plenty of time to turn around. All these thoughts flooded my mind, but I knew it was time to put on my big girl pants and face what I'd been avoiding.

- They'll know I haven't been to church.
- They'll judge me.
- They'll be too pushy.
- They'll be too preachy.
- They are all saved; where do I fit in?

At that moment, I had the biggest decision to make. Do I give in to my human feelings and assumptions, or do I follow through with what I think my spirit is being called to? It was down to Him (God) or me. You see how far "I" had gotten me. What if He had something better in store than I could ever imagine? So, I chose God! I took a deep breath, got my family out of the car, and walked toward the door.

You'd be surprised that there wasn't any finger pointing, staring, or shaming. The images we paint in our minds amaze me. Instead, we were greeted by so many people with genuine smiles. The "Ask Me For Help" purple shirt team escorted us over to the children's ministry area, explained the process, and we were all checked in. We smelled the aroma of fresh, hot coffee and heard laughter and joy-filled conversations. My husband and I looked at each other in amazement. Was it too good to be true?

While getting coffee (who misses out on fresh, free coffee? Not this girl!), we heard the band begin to play. My ears heard something that caught their attention, live vocalists leading worship. I used to enjoy singing and writing music but had given it up when I became heartbroken over the loss of our first son. My joy and songbird died along with him. At that point, I had not recovered.

It was time to find a seat, and yes, we went through the "let's not sit too close to the front, maybe in the middle, or the back" conversation. I know it seems like a bit much, but I didn't want to be seen. "Let's just be lowkey," is what I thought. It was crazy to even try to do this because, guess what, we were one of the only minority families in the room. Did they make us feel that way? Of course not. Did we feel that way? Of course, we did.

The point of giving you this background information is that I want you to see it was a process. I am human, and I have been there, just like you. I have been in a rut with overwhelming feelings, but the best part is if I can do it, so can you.

Fast forward to November. It was my first year being away from my family, so I promised them I would come home for Thanksgiving and Christmas. I had never flown before (crazy me), so I drove fourteen hours with my four-year-old son back to Virginia. Remember, my husband and I were at odds. I didn't pressure him to go. No need to ruin the trip with us being awkward and uncomfortable with each other, right?

Little did I know, this plan was unfolding just as God had intended. I was about to be confronted by the Alpha and Omega Himself. The Savior, our King, our Father, had a divine appointment set for me, and I was oblivious.

I'll never forget this encounter. It was painful, but it changed my life!

While driving in the middle of the night, I decided to put on my Christian music. I had learned a few new songs since attending the new church. I also had some favorites that I had not played in a while.

I was singing along, praising, and suddenly, I heard, "It's you."

What?! "It's you?" I glanced back to see if my son was saying something, but of course, he was sleeping. I paused for a moment and turned the music down. I questioned back, "It's me?"

The time had come to hear the truth. I had been initially praying for my marriage, but as the weeks went on, I had started praying that God would fix me. I wanted Him to change whoever I'd become and show me who I really could be. What was I doing praying boldly like that right out the gate? In my women's group, I had learned about praying dangerously and wondered if or how that would work. Well, I was about to find out. The spotlight's now on me.

"When was the last time you sent sweet messages to your husband?"

"How are you going to ask him to love you when you don't even love yourself?"

"How can he love someone who cuts down everything in the way?"

"When was the last time you were a wife?"

Wait a moment, this was getting personal. I had the ring. I had the paper. We were married. I am his wife.

God said, "I'll ask you again. When was the last time you were a wife?"

Only one word could describe this moment: speechless.

"You're not a wife. You're a provider. You pay the bills. You order everyone around. Yes, they have food and shelter, but what's better than love?"

I felt the heaviness of these words so much I almost had to pull over. "You're not a wife. You're a provider." There is a difference between the two.

This is what I wanted to reply...

- He never listens.
- He doesn't act as if he cares.
- He is lazy.
- He doesn't help me at all.

Did I ever give him a chance? God was telling me all the things that no one wants to hear, and all I could say was...

"Yes, Lord, I take full responsibility for my actions. Forgive me and show me the way."

I immediately started texting my husband about our favorite songs and memories. I told him that I missed us. We were best friends and had now become two people so distant from each other. We were just putting up with the day-to-day life.

When my husband saw the messages, he didn't respond by saying, "Me too." He asked, " Are you feeling okay?" That hit me like a ton of bricks. I knew then God was right. The time had come for me to save myself and save my marriage. I was in an uncomfortable place.

Showing vulnerability was never my thing, but it is how we should be with God and those closest to us.

I knew all of this would never make sense via text, so I told him we would discuss it later and that I loved him. Wow, I had just texted my husband, and it felt like I was texting a stranger. Also, it seemed like I was pulling rose petals off a flower–he loves me, he loves me not, he loves me.

What a predicament!

The craziest thing happened after that, though. I began to feel again. It was like an old clock starting to turn for the first time. I felt like I could hear my heartbeat again. My eyes were wide open, and I believe I even felt a little joy. I rarely smiled until then, unless it was forced.

With this one act of accepting who I'd allowed myself to become, I no longer had that chain attached. There was no stronghold anymore. So, that's how it works?

My job then was to take heed to God's word, to walk through the door He was opening, and continue to build this new life I was seeking. There was a hard lesson to learn in this moment, but I pray it helps you reflect and heal not only your marriage but also those broken friendships or family relationships.

Forgiveness is the key to uprooting bitterness!

Take responsibility for your actions, your words, and the things you are not so proud of, and just like that, you remove the weapon the enemy has been using against you. You've pulled his card.

You're not going to be perfect. You're still going to stumble. Getting back up is always the hardest part, but God is willing to be there if you allow Him.

No one has ever said you must do it alone. I guarantee it is just your pride talking. Find a community of people within the church, your discipleship group, to do life with. You'll learn we all have our skeletons, but we are becoming better for it.

God knows you. He created you. He knows what you've done. He has forgiven you, but are you willing to forgive yourself?

- You're worthy.
- You deserve to be happy.
- You deserve to be in His presence.

YOU CAN DO IT!

Humble yourself before Him. I took the responsibility, I took up my cross, will you?

Matthew 16:24-25

"If any of you want to be my followers, you must give up your own way, take up your cross, and follow me. If you try to hang on to your life, you will lose it but if you give up your life for my sake, you will save it." (NLT)

James 4:6-8

"And he gives grace generously. As the Scriptures say, 'God opposes the proud but gives grace to the humble.' So humble yourselves before God. Resist the devil, and he will flee from you. Come close to God, and God will come close to you." (NLT)

Notes

Prayers

CHAPTER SIX

Is This My Order?

Unexpected Turn

Hanging out in a coffee shop is so interesting. Everyone is meeting in one common area and sharing a common interest but racing out the door in totally different directions. I've noticed that some smile and say hello, and some stay on their phones with their heads down, wanting to get in and out as quickly as possible. All I can think about with the person who keeps their head down is how much energy it takes them to disengage from their surroundings. I can feel the tension it is bringing between wanting to engage but not really. It reminds me of the roller coaster of life, the tension between getting the best news of your life and then being hit with the worst news of your life at the same time.

My husband and I have been riding this roller coaster of life together since we were twenty-one. It amazes me the things we have endured during our time together, but I tell you, they have made us so much more resilient. We look back now, laugh, and thank God that we had each other and Him to help us make it through. We were married in October 2010, and being so young, we had only spoken about having children in passing. He joked about wanting three children because he had siblings, and then there was me, the only child, who thought he was crazy.

Another reason I had not considered something so serious was that he was living in a different city at the time. We met online and were traveling back and forth to be with each other. When we were married, we didn't have the careers we have now or savings. We had love, hope, and prayer. I was living with my mom, and he was living with his grandmother. My mom wanted us to continue living with her, but we opted to finally find a place together. Most would have stayed with family, but we found out some news that made us act quickly.

One morning, I woke up and was not feeling well. My husband was back home, and I was on my way to hang out with my sister (my best friend). At the time, I thought nothing of it, but eventually, my intuition told me that I needed to head to the nearest store. So, there I was, alone in the pharmacy line, picking out a home pregnancy test, and thinking, "It can't be. I have goals, I am in school, we don't live together, I can't be a mother, and my life is over." Yes, these were my actual thoughts at twenty-four years old.

I took the test while I was still at the pharmacy, and to my surprise, there it was, those little pink lines that can cause either celebration or panic. At the time, it caused a complete panic attack. I sat in my car, freaking out for at least thirty minutes. I called my sister, and she said, "It's going to be alright, don't worry, just breathe." As always, that is easier said than done. I went to pick up my sister and called my husband, and at first, he did not respond as I thought he would, especially since he was the one who initially wanted children. I look back on that now, and I think we were both in shock, our emotions were high, and we knew we needed to figure it all out. We had mere months of marriage under our belt, and now we were adding parenting to the list.

My husband eventually moved to Richmond, and we began preparing for our newest addition. We found out that we were having a son. We began searching for names, and for some reason, my husband, who was in love with the show *Lost*, could not shake the name Dezmond. I couldn't agree to it right away, but it was a contender.

One afternoon, I was lying in bed, and I told my husband something wasn't feeling right, so I laid down for a bit. Once I got up, I did feel a bit better, but it was still unsettling. My friend had called to let me know that her brother had just had his first child, and she wanted me to ride with her to the hospital. I agreed to go with her to celebrate and figured it would take my mind off of panicking. When we arrived at the hospital to see her brother, I almost told her that I was going to check myself into the ED, but then I thought, "Maybe I am overreacting." Everything went fine at the hospital, and as soon as I returned home, I laid back down. I reassured myself that we had just had our ultrasound and vaginal check, everything was looking fine, and the baby's heartbeat was strong.

During the time of my pregnancy, I had been working in a hospital as an IV Pharmacy Technician. I loved this job and my co-workers. It always felt like I was having such a direct impact on our patients' care. It was a highlight of my pharmacy career.

I arrived to work the next morning, and all of a sudden, I could barely walk. It felt like there was a bubble between my legs. I sat down and told the pharmacist that we might need to call OB to come get me.

I was wheeled off to the OB floor, and everyone was so welcoming; we all knew each other. I was checked in and began to call family. My doctor came over, and they began running tests and checking out everything. All the waiting made me anxious, and I wondered what the bubble feeling was that had made me need to sit. As the doctors talked in the hallway, I had this eerie feeling they were about to give me some bad news. Finally, my doctor came in with the specialist, and they told me that my water bag had dropped through my cervix. I was experiencing what they call Incompetent Cervix. Incompetent Cervix is when your body hits the second trimester and the baby gets heavier, but your cervix becomes weak, causing premature labor. I had never heard of this in my life. Now the question was, how do we fix this and save my baby? "We wait," they said.

I couldn't believe they were telling me that the only way to save my son was to sit on bed rest in the hospital and wait to see if I could make it to at least twenty-three weeks. At the time, I was eighteen going on nineteen weeks pregnant, so that time felt like millions of years away. At this point, I was not prepared for all of this, and what about my job? Lucky for me, my Pharmacy Director was very understanding.

We made it through the first night, which was a miracle. My nurses began tilting my bed to make me look like I was upside down. The hope was that maybe gravity would begin working and move the bag back into place. Our son's fluids were doing pretty well, there were no concerns yet. I looked pretty funny to my visitors as they came into the room, but I couldn't care less. I would have allowed them to hang me upside down from anything they asked if it meant saving our child.

Time passed, I continued to pray, and the doctors continued to think of ways to help, but one thing was for certain—being on the cusp of celebration and death was not easy. There were many days I cried and began guilt tripping myself, thinking it was my fault, and my body was a failure. Then there were days I had settled into believing this was just a moment in time, and we were going to beat this.

The day before our lives changed, one doctor came into our room and stated that my fluid levels had dropped, and we should start thinking about our next steps. I was shocked that this doctor wanted me to give up, and at that moment, she was not my favorite person. She told me there was a risky surgery they could try called a cerclage. She wanted to take me to the OR, push the bag back in, then tie a stitch around my cervix to have the pregnancy move forward. At twenty-four, you'd think that was enough to scare you right out of the bed, and it did. This surgery meant no more waiting, and if she popped the bag, which was very likely, his little life would be over right then. I opted to wait, and I am glad I did because we made it a whole week more after that.

I was moved from the OB wing to a full-time stay unit. I wasn't hooked up to many medications and had all that I needed. I wasn't even allowed to get out of the bed to go to the restroom, which I appreciated because I was too afraid to move most days.

On the first night in the other room, my husband and I put on our show and decided to order pizza. I couldn't wait for it to get there since it was my favorite meal. Little did I know, this pizza would be the last meal that my little guy and I would share.

While eating the pizza, I felt a tickle in my throat. I hadn't coughed once since being in the hospital, and now this was happening. I was trying to hold the cough in because I knew how sensitive my situation was. I didn't want to impact anything, but the cough was still persistent. I tried to sip some of my drink, hold my breath, you name it. Nothing was working at this point, and before I knew it, there was a full-blown cough. One single cough changed everything. At that very moment, my water broke, and I knew we were in the final hours. Everyone kept reassuring me that this didn't mean anything, but I knew. I knew that I had messed up any chance of my son surviving. All because of a slice of pizza.

The next morning, I kept feeling like I had to use the restroom, but nothing was coming out. You all know what happened next–pain that hit like no other. I was in active labor, and everyone was rushing around but also asking me to remain calm. What a thing to ask me at this moment, it felt like I was having an out-of-body experience. I asked my husband to call our families and let them know what was going on. My heart was then, and is still today as I write this, breaking into a million pieces.

There was nothing they could do to stop what was happening. I was given medication for the pain, but my doctor explained that at nineteen weeks and four days, there was nothing they could do to save his life. The strong heartbeat that I heard every day, the kicks, and then they told me he was not going to make it, plus called him a miscarriage? No, I still don't agree with that label. His name is Dezmond, he was our baby, he was living, and he is the reason our lives changed forever.

At the time, I couldn't see God working. I was clouded with hurt, shame, disgust, and disbelief. I wasn't an every Sunday churchgoer, but I knew He was my God. I questioned Him for almost four hours after my son was born until his last breath. Why me? Why us? Why Dezmond? It didn't make sense then, but I see now that it was for this very purpose. To show others that have suffered such a tremendous loss that God is faithful in the valley. He will supply all our needs in His timing. I was not alone, even though it felt like it. He needed our son for a purpose. Dezmond struck something within me that I never knew I wanted or needed: the desire to be a mother.

Lamentations 3:22-24

"The steadfast love of the Lord never
ceases; his mercies never come to
an end; they are new every morning;
great is your faithfulness. 'The
Lord is my portion,' says my soul,
'therefore I will hope in him.'" (ESV)

Notes

Notes

Prayers

_____
_____
_____
_____
_____
_____
_____
_____
_____
_____
_____
_____
_____
_____
_____
_____
_____
_____
_____
_____
_____
_____
_____

CHAPTER SEVEN

Running on Empty

The War on Worship

"One Adonai Latte for Shena," God calls. Hand stretched out to grab the cup, I begin to think, am I ready or deserving to accept it? Let's look back at when I first got to the church.

During service, announcements were made about different ways you could connect to the church. This seemed like a good idea, but I had just gotten there, and wasn't I trying to hide or be low-key? Well, I took the leap and joined a women's group that same week. Our first meeting was on a Wednesday.

As I look back over this journey, I have noticed that God does not make it easy. He always finds a way to make me uncomfortable. It works out in the end, but man, that first step is very uncomfortable.

When I walked into the meeting room, I thought, "Here we go. Whispers are going to start, and they will probably stare." Crazy things will run through your head when you are nervous, don't judge me. I was greeted by what seemed like an angel. I swear she had the most infectious, warm smile. She introduced herself, and I felt very comfortable for some reason. She was the women's group leader. So far, so good. We went around saying our names, they shared the purpose of the group, and then we began our discussion. Little did I know, the tides were about to turn, and if you think walking into the room was the most uncomfortable part, think again.

The group leader announced that we were going to split into groups, talk, and pray for each other. I felt like I was being thrown off a ledge with no parachute. Did she just ask me to pray for someone out loud? Did she just say I need to tell someone my issues? Where is the door?! My idea of a women's group was just studying the Word and having the people, who have been in ministry longer, pray over us. What was a broken woman like me going to do for someone else? I am a mess, and this is not the time to think that my prayers can move mountains.

I couldn't make a run for it, but I did think of faking an illness. I laugh now, but my invisible collar was getting very tight. The group leader put me in a group with herself and two other women. We went into this little classroom off to the side of the main room, a children's ministry room. It was so cute with the colorful little chairs and miniature tables. It tickled me that we were about to discuss major things in such an interesting place.

The group leader asked me for my name again and wanted me to tell everyone a little about myself–traditional introduction for a new girl. I let them know that I had just moved to Florida on September 1st from Richmond, Virginia. I was given the name of the church by someone, who used to attend, that I knew from my hometown. I was married, had a son who was four years old at the time, and I hadn't been to church in years but felt God had told me that it was time to return. They were all happy to hear that. They also knew my friend from my hometown and had wonderful things to say about her and her husband. They introduced themselves and explained how long they had been coming to the church. It was nice to hear that they had found their home there. We had been delayed for a bit, and the group leader asked if anyone wanted to share what had been on their heart. I was thinking in my mind, "Honey, we are going to need longer than this hour together to work through this black heart of mine."

One lady spoke up by raising her hand and saying, "I'll go." I thought, "How brave of her to go first." She began explaining her story about her husband and family, then the group leader chimed in about hers, tears were now falling, and I was blown away. I thought to myself, "Hold on, these ladies, who attend church regularly, have real-world problems like mine?" It was refreshing that this was a safe space. They were not judging each other. It was therapeutic.

After hearing them speak, everyone wiped their wet eyes and snotty noses. Then the unthinkable had to happen. They asked for my story. Well, you already know how that went. I explained how my relationship with my husband was two steps away from being a divorce. I told them I moved there for my job and had given him an ultimatum. I explained that I was in a dark place and hadn't quite healed from the loss of my son a few years earlier. I had just given up on happiness and connecting with anyone. I believed in God because I was taught that at a young age, but I did not have a relationship with Him—well, not like I was supposed to have. They reassured me that it does get better and I was in the right place. These ladies were hearing things about my life that I had never shared with anyone. Sometimes all you need is a new perspective and a little bit of holy sprinkled on a situation to figure out that the valley has been walked before, and you will get through it.

We got a reminder that it was almost time to worship, so we should probably wrap up. I froze instantly. We were not going on stage, right? Am I going to have to sing with this group? I do not have a voice. It was locked away somewhere, frozen in time. The group leader explained that they normally sneak into band practice sometimes, or if there is a worship set going on, they attend. God, how many things can you make me face at once? It was a lot for my first week of trying to be a Christian.

The group leader then said, "Let's take turns praying for each other, then we will go." I thought for sure we had forgotten all about that. I openly admitted that I had never prayed out loud for anyone before, and I had stopped singing out loud years ago. I had never worshiped freely. They were compassionate about this and told me that I didn't have to this time, but maybe I could give it a try next time. The keyword was try. They decided to pray over me that day, and I had never had that happen either. I remember when the first words started coming to my ears that I had this weird feeling on the inside. It is hard to describe, but think about giving your car a jump. The motor tries to turn over, and the car shakes a bit. Let me just say I was trying to hold in the ugliest cry I had ever had in my life, and I do not cry. What were they doing to me? I knew then that something inside me was trying to wake up. I felt something stirring. I had no clue what it was, but after crying, I felt a bit better.

We went to worship, and of course, they walked to the front row. I was next to the group leader and again felt like I was having an out-of-body experience. I looked around, and almost everyone had their hands raised and was singing. I felt out of place. The group leader whispered to me, "Give it a try." I couldn't open my mouth or lift my hands. It felt like my tongue was locked to the bottom of my mouth, and my hands were shackled to the chair. This is what you call a stronghold. The enemy had control of my mouth and my hands. He had muted me for so long that I did not know how to release it. At the end of the meeting, we gave hugs and left for the night. I returned the next week, and that's when I began thinking, "You know what, I shouldn't ask God to fix my marriage. I need to ask God to fix me first."

Worship is one of the best weapons we have, along with prayer. The enemy can control our thoughts, and he, for sure, can intercept them. It is the only control he believes he has. He can fill our minds with crazy, unwanted, negative things, but it is always up to us to say, "Not today, Satan." I had vowed and almost made a pledge that the enemy took to heart. He probably had a celebration the day that he finally got one from God's flock. But he didn't know that it would only be temporary.

This war on worship was actually a war on my purpose. It was hard to move past. Little did I know that I was missing out on so much by allowing myself to shrink down and be closed off from speaking, singing, praying, and worshipping. I couldn't see how they were all connected. I didn't know at the time that it was hindering me from truly knowing God. All I knew was I was hurting and didn't feel like it, and that was good enough for me. This is another reason why we should be in a community with other believers. We need someone to call us out on this. We need someone in our corner to pray when we cannot, to go to war when we cannot, to stand up when we cannot, to ask God to bring His presence when we cannot, to say, "Girl, get it together. We will make it through this."

I didn't let go of this stronghold on the first day, the second week, the first month, or the third month. I started with just standing during worship, and then I began to sway a little one day. This was my worship, and I know God was saying, "You're almost home." As time went on, I began to tap my fingers–I was getting feeling back in my hands. I started to hum along with the songs. No words were being said, but I was working my way to it. The next time, I let go of the chair and held my hands with my fingers intertwined. Slowly but surely, I released my hands and let my arms bend enough that I could hold my palms up to my waist. I even tried putting one hand halfway up. All of this was preparing me for the day that I would humble myself and stop worrying about who was looking, how I was looking, or even if this was how to worship. I gave it my best.

I even remember finally getting to raise my hands and thinking I had won the battle. I decided that I was going to step out in faith and ask to be on the worship team. I hadn't considered that they would actually want to put me on stage with a mic, as I knew I still had a lot of work to do. But they did. I was put back in the children's ministry area as they had a music team also. It was just a shadow day, but the worship leader handed me a mic, and I wouldn't take it. She laid it on the table and said, "Take your time. When you're ready, feel free to join in."

What a process! If you met me now, you wouldn't know any of this happened. I am the crazy lady in service who is singing loudly, swaying, raising my hands, and almost making motions to the songs. I let my spirit take over. You may even see me jumping up and down with my hair swinging. It depends on the song. Don't play "Rattle" by Elevation Worship unless you want me to show out, and if you want to see my heart pour out, you may want to play "Graves into Gardens," "Wait on You," or "Jireh." The list could go on. God saved me, and there is nothing that I wouldn't do to worship in front of His throne.

The enemy had cornered me and thought he won. I can't deny it. There is no other way to describe it. I had permanently muted myself, and it was all he ever wanted. See, the enemy knows who we are in Heaven. He knows we have a purpose, and he does not want us to find out what it may be.

I wanted to share this to say that voice that you hear that says, you sound terrible, they don't want to hear you, God isn't listening, your prayers don't have power, they are laughing at you, you don't have what it takes, don't stand up, no one else is doing it–please don't believe it. This is your time to break free and say, you know what, I have had enough of being cornered and silenced. I can do this. My worship is not for anyone else but God, and He knows me better than anyone. He sees my flaws. If He wanted me to be like everyone else, then you know what, He would have made that happen. You are original, and there is only one you that is divinely created for a purpose that only God knows. Community in the church is there to guide you, love you, and show you how to get to that purpose. In this war, you must know when to say enough is enough. I am in control, and there is nothing more this enemy can take from me. I want to know who God says that I am. Face it and break the chains. You are powerful. You are what Heaven needs. Your worship could be the key to the next blessing that will be poured out. Someone may be waiting to see someone like them raise their hands. You can influence the room. Just give it a try.

Ephesians 6:13-19

"Therefore, put on every piece of God's armor so you will be able to resist the enemy in the time of evil. Then after the battle you will still be standing firm. Stand your ground, putting on the belt of truth and the body armor of God's righteousness. For shoes, put on the peace that comes from the Good News so that you will be fully prepared. In addition to all of these, hold up the shield of faith to stop the fiery arrows of the devil. Put on salvation as your helmet, and take the sword of the Spirit, which is the word of God. Pray in the Spirit at all times and on every occasion. Stay alert and be persistent in your prayers for all believers everywhere." (NLT)

Notes

Prayers

CHAPTER EIGHT

A Sample of the Finest Roast

The Heart to Serve

Fragrant but just like sweet sugar browning, dripping with honey, topped with whipped cream, and swirled with caramel because He knows me better than I know myself. It was the most beautiful cup of coffee I had ever seen. I call it the Elohim Frappuccino. He knew it would prepare me for what was next, serving His Kingdom.

Since I've fully given my life back to Christ, I've learned there is something so special about the word serve. I am not going to act like I completely understood it at first, but I quickly learned that it was something I truly enjoyed. As I spoke before, I wasn't comfortable being in the spotlight, but God didn't hear that at all. He immediately began attacking this stronghold so that I could serve in the capacity that He needed me to.

I've also learned that a lot of what God calls us to is not for us. We may be able to learn something from the situation, but it is more about what we can do for the vine.

What fruit can we produce for the Kingdom? It is about finding your place in the body of Christ and always being willing to be an open vessel.

Sometimes, when we are broken, we can think that there is nothing else to give, but I promise that laying your feelings down for a moment will be so worth it. Serving is a true act of God. Serving is an act of reverence. It is all about your heart posture and your willingness to see past your desires and serve those in need of His love, His community.

My heart to serve came from a place of thanks. When God began to change me from the inside out, I felt a calling to do more. A calling to humbly show Him how grateful I was for all that He had done for me. Yes, we can pray and tithe, but sometimes we need a more personal touch.

You can imagine my surprise when God placed me in an area that I didn't EVER think I would want to be in, children's ministry. Don't judge me too quickly, but I never thought that I could work with children. They are all little people with different personalities, and the biggest part is that they didn't belong to me. What was I going to do in such a setting? I was petrified. I also had a chip on my shoulder. It wasn't the church's fault, but remember, I was still trying to come down from the pedestal that I had placed myself on. The persona that I had developed was so arrogant that it all seemed beneath me. I did not see the blessing in this at all. I was still blinded by who I thought I was and believed they should know who they were in front of. I kept thinking about the fact that they wanted me to jump around and dance with children–it felt like such an embarrassment at first. I know it sounds terrible, but that was me. I am so glad God didn't give up on me and that I pushed through.

Let's fast forward a bit because you'd never guess where I am now. I am now the Kids Ministry Worship Team Lead. Yes, the complaining girl you just read about spends every waking moment in the children's ministry area, and I LOVE IT. These children bless me way more than I could ever bless them. The love they pour into my life is genuine and could never be duplicated. I am overwhelmed with emotion as I write this. They are such a joy, and just thinking of my selfishness and how I almost missed out on being with them blows my mind, but it is all a part of the process.

These kids are such a vital part of my life, my faith, and my journey. They come in every Sunday ready to bring it big and give their hearts to God. If you've never seen it up close, please visit your local church and ask how you can participate. Many think that kids don't understand, but when I say they pray, they sing with all their hearts, and they love Jesus, trust me, there is no doubt God is with them. I just can't believe I get to take part in this. I am forever grateful, and I thank God daily that He chose me for such a precious duty. Your impact will last well past Sunday morning. I see these kids in the local store, and they are running to me and saying, "Mrs. Shena, Mrs. Shena," and I don't take that for granted.

I've grown to realize that sometimes our greatest gifts from God never come in the way we expect them to. This opportunity for a blessing went against everything I knew, thought, or felt, but I agreed when I didn't understand. I agreed when I couldn't see the full picture. He is the author and artist, developing each masterpiece one stroke at a time. We can get little glimpses into His vision, but we must stay the course for the big reveal.

Through all of this, I am so proud to say that I would do it all over again a million times to be a part of these children and their families' lives, to sacrifice so that they can meet with God freely. Children are where it all begins. Their little hearts are waiting to be directed the right way. Why wouldn't we want to direct them towards the love of the greatest Father?

As I have grown in my love to serve and my responsibilities, I not only uprooted my family to move to Florida, but I also told my husband that we were leaving our apartment to move closer to the church. At first, he didn't understand, but I told him it had to be done. I get questioned all the time by people about the decision. "You moved for a church?" they ask. YES! I moved for a church, and I have seen people move for reasons that are not as valid as this. We can't just see it as a building. This was the place where God embraced me and gave me a new life. This was the place of forgiveness. This was where I was rebuilt. This was my first moment of truly getting to know who I am. There is no other place I would rather be. I want to be available at any moment He may need me, and living thirty minutes away was way too far, in my opinion. I pray I keep this in my spirit for many years to come. If He never lets go, I'll never let go. If He promises to meet me there, I'll be there. Until He changes my direction, this is home. He needs something from me in this place of worship, and I need something as well.

Serving is a choice, and I'll choose Him every time. It is a sacrifice that we must be willing to make. We could never repay what He has done for us, but we can always try with a hallelujah and a life on mission to help bring Heaven to earth as He intended. I challenge you to pray with intention and ask, "How can I be of service to you, Lord?" It is our duty and birthright.

Matthew 5:14-16

"Your lives light up the world. For how can you hide a city that stands on a hilltop? And who would light a lamp and then hide it in an obscure place? Instead, it's placed where everyone in the house can benefit from its light. So don't hide your light! Let it shine brightly before others so that your commendable works will shine as light upon them, and then they will give their praise to your Father in heaven." (TPT)

Notes

Notes

Prayers

CHAPTER NINE

He Leads Me to the Cup

Avoiding the Call

"This cup is perfect for you, but it is up to you how you choose to fill it." - God

We have been on a ride throughout this book so far. I hope you have refreshed your coffee, or if you aren't a coffee drinker, then your favorite beverage. I want to address another issue that was prominent throughout this story, or my testimony, I should say: avoiding the call. I avoided it like the plague. Not just the call to faith, but everything.

I have found myself questioning, why does it have to be this way? Why would I want to put myself in this predicament? What is needed of me now? The biggest question of them all, why me? It's because God can bring us to the cup, but He lets us choose how we fill it. He guides us to the correct choice through His Holy Spirit.

I will be honest; God has said some scary things to me. He has asked me to take some leaps, and I think, who does He truly think I am? He cannot be talking to me. The one thing I have learned is that God is one persistent Father.

When I say He repeats, I mean He brings on messages with the same theme everywhere, wakes me up faithfully at 3:00 a.m. to get my attention, and speaks through others with the same message until I make a move. I often wonder why it seems that He doesn't allow time to ask for a second opinion or seek counsel on the newfound desires of His heart. Sometimes I just need a moment to think it through first. God does not like to be delayed, and it is understandable. Most of the time, He wants us to make moves because someone needs us or maybe a place needs us.

God's call is different from any other voice. I can immediately tell when He wants my attention or needs me to switch directions. Of course, it wasn't always that way, and I give credit to Priscilla Shirer. Thank you so much for writing *Discerning the Voice of God*. My goodness, that book changed my life. If you haven't read it, get it. It explained so much of what I was feeling and how to block out the nonsense to focus on Him.

Let's discuss some of the things that I avoided the call on. I hopefully have a lot more life to live, so I know this list will grow.

- God has given me the blueprint for a whole ministry.
- I delayed the birth of my son Jaxon for four years.
- I didn't write this book until now but started having the calling a couple of years ago.
- God has been saying, "Let go, make room, obey, the time is now," for over a year.

The problem with all of this is confidence and belief in myself. Truly, I ask every day, Lord, are you sure people want to hear from me? I have not been faithfully following You for as long as most have. I do not know every Bible verse. I do not know the exact year of Exodus, Jonah being in the whale, or Noah building the Ark. I don't know every single major or minor prophet, nor have I read the Bible in its entirety from cover to cover, but what I do have is a heart for Jesus. I must constantly remind myself that the disciples in the Bible did not have divinity degrees or titles. They were fishermen, a tax collector, and broken and lost people who decided, "I want to follow Him." Jesus taught them the ways of living for God. He is the ultimate example.

I have found that I am not alone in this feeling. Some of us walk around thinking we need to be perfect for God to love us or for Him to call us to something greater. I have learned that no matter what I am feeling or thinking, God will continue pushing me out of my comfort zone and towards what He needs or wants. Although it seems scary and doesn't make sense at the time, we can always feel sure that God has gone before us and prepared the way. I am not making this up as I go. I am just applying all that He has spoken in the Bible, His Word, His truth.

Another word you may hear that defines avoiding a call is delayed obedience. My, my, that sounds worse than avoiding the call. Well, they both leave something to be desired. God has been beating me down for over a year about obeying. Remember what I said about the repetition of what He wants? Every time I hear a message or look around, we are right back at the same topic. Yes, I got saved and gave my life back to Christ, but I am still looking over the edge and saying, "This jump is way too high." My prayer is always that He forgives me for delaying. This new walk that I am on terrifies me sometimes.

As you may have noticed above, I had stated that I was avoiding a call I received about my new son, Jaxon. My goodness, this little man lights up my life. He was born in June 2020, right at the heart of the pandemic. No, he wasn't supposed to be a pandemic baby, but hey, we had no clue at the end of 2019 that everything was going to change. This is a prime example of God knowing where our lives are going and us being unaware.

I had started having dreams of a child years before. It was always the same dream. My son, Jaiden, and I were at a park or backyard. I could never see the whole setting, but I knew we were outside. The only thing I could hear myself saying each time was, "Jaiden, go get your brother." Every time I woke up, I would think, "What brother?" Dezmond died before Jaiden was born, and this seemed like a younger brother. Right before we got pregnant with Jaxon, everyone at church was having a baby, then all of a sudden, my close friends were saying we were next. I kept denying it because there was no way I wanted to go through that again.

I have a condition called Incompetent Cervix. It was the cause of my loss with Dezmond. What happens is my body gets to the second trimester, and my cervix begins to soften. My body goes into premature labor–it sounds like my body is working against me. Well, in order to save my second son and Jaxon, I needed to have a cerclage placed to hold my cervix together. Yes, a string is sewn through my cervix and pulled tight enough to hold a growing baby for nine months. If the loss of a child wasn't enough to delay a thought about having another child, then having to go through this surgery should be.

I went to the doctor in August or September of 2019 because it was time to renew my IUD. TMI for some that may be reading, but it is needed to get the full picture. My awesome OB/GYN came in to see me; she was always the best to converse with. I couldn't wait to see her. I was there thinking, "This is going to be quick. Hopefully, it doesn't hurt, and then I am out of here." But it did not exactly go that way. She began to ask me why I had not had any other children, and I explained the situation. She said, "Girl, you know I specialize in high-risk pregnancy." I couldn't believe she was saying this. It was coming from all directions at this point. She then informed me that I was getting older, and there was no better time than then. Oh yes, I know, an African American female, who is heading towards her mid-thirties, seems like time is running out. I informed her that my husband had always wanted more children, but my anxiety over trying and having to have surgery again had always deterred me from it.

Here came the tricky part. She offered me an ultimatum. I could put the IUD in, and it would be another six years before I could try for another child, or she could just remove it, and we could see what would happen. That took a complete left turn. She said she would give me a few minutes to think about it. I began to shake so much that I could barely think or talk. I couldn't believe I was at this crossroads. I knew what I felt like God was telling me, but I also knew what I didn't want to do. I didn't want the opportunity to be hurt again. I was doing so well, and we were healing. I was scared to backtrack, but God said, "Trust Me, I've got this." I called my husband in the office, sitting on the examination table, and told him what she said. He freaked a little and put the ball back in my court. We debated if we could do it and then said, "It is now or never, right?" If this is what God said, we should see.

My doctor came back, and I told her, "Okay, let's just remove it, and we will see what happens. If it doesn't take before my follow-up appointment, have my IUD ready." She removed it, and I left the office feeling vulnerable and confused but also a little bit tickled that I did it. I had finally done something God asked of me that was completely against my beliefs. As time went on, it was an easier pill to swallow. The good news is that God was correct. Just weeks later, we had a positive test. The anxiety didn't stop there, as we had also had a D&C before. We went to our eight-week appointment, and there he was. Yes, I was the only one who was confident that my new baby was a boy. God had said it, and so I knew it was so. He had also told me that my son, Jaiden, was a boy. I didn't tell everyone how I knew, but I did.

Since I let go and let God, He showed me that when He says, "I am in the fire," He truly is. When He says, "I've got it," don't second guess. When He calls, we need to answer. When He says, "This is what I am calling you to, and there is no one else better," we should believe it. Jax filled a void that I didn't even know existed. I was so shocked at how our family came together when he was born.

I have a lot to learn about having the faith of the first disciples, the "I will do anything crazy for Jesus" type of faith. Well, crazy to me, but not crazy to Him. The twelve disciples are the ultimate example of true faith. Okay, let's not count Judas. He is one to be left out. Yes, they questioned, but for the most part, they preached the good news even though they could be harmed, put in jail, killed, or even put out of their families. We have so much more freedom today, but we still hesitate to listen or move when God says to. I am thankful for them and thankful for Paul, who was ultimately on an opposite path and decided to change his ways. Did you know he was tasked with killing Christians? He gave us so much in the New Testament. God used him for so much good, and He can use you too.

Ephesians 5:17

"Don't act thoughtlessly, but understand what the Lord wants you to do." (NLT)

1 Thessalonians 5:24

"The one who calls you is faithful, and he will do it." (NIV)

Notes

Notes

Prayers

CHAPTER TEN

Who's Doing the Pouring?

Turn Hobbies into Habits

"I'll take a refill, please."

I am here waiting patiently for more, but there is quite a line. The first thing that crosses my mind is, who's doing the pouring? I sometimes feel convicted by the things that I say or think. This made me realize that I could dig deeper into this, so I put on my Christian lenses, the lenses that bring logic and help me see things a bit clearer. Honestly, it feels like I am wearing 3D vision, and those thought bubbles tend to pop up to help me clarify the situation. It guides me on which part of my new Christian characteristics I should apply at this moment. I see a thought bubble that says faith, wisdom, love, compassion, all the qualities that God has placed in our hearts. I find it is easier to ask the Holy Spirit how to know which to select. The slight prompting to lean one way or the other normally shows me the way. While I wait, let's discuss hobbies and habits.

How many times in your life have you been asked what your hobbies are? For me, too many to count! I wonder, though, why no one ever asks what your habits are? Maybe it's because hobbies have more of a fun nature. When you hear the word hobbies, you immediately begin thinking of things you enjoy doing.

- Knitting
- Painting
- Drawing
- Writing
- Running

I had to name a few, so you can get the picture. When we hear the word habits, we cringe a little. Habits are those things in life that we cling to and are hard to get rid of. They are the things that can hinder us or cripple our potential sometimes.

Habits, such as:

- Drinking too much
- Lying
- Cursing
- Rushing
- Surfing social media for hours
- Blaming others
- Being controlling

Don't get me wrong, there are good habits as well:

- Brushing your teeth
- Regularly exercising
- Setting a schedule to ensure you're rested
- Cleaning

- Being punctual
- Being responsible with money (saving, 401k, giving God His first portion!)

There must be a good balance between hobbies and habits. Think about this, where would your faith or beliefs fall? Do you make God a priority, or is He just an occasional hobby? I have to say that for most of my life, I was a hobbyist. I had surface-level faith.

- I thanked God for waking me up.
- I thanked God for my food.
- I tuned into church online sometimes.
- I did whatever I wanted to do.
- I owned multiple Bibles and never read one.
- I prayed when times were hard.
- I prayed when I wanted the promotion.
- I prayed when I wanted favor.

Now...

- I thank God EVERY DAY for saving me.
- I thank God for new life and grace in abundance.
- I pray not only for myself but for those around me.
- I ask God to allow me into His throne room.
- I rebuke the devil with confidence (He's got to come a better way than the usual!).
- I listen to be called or directed by God.
- I make church and God a HABIT.

For one moment, imagine if God treated us like a hobby, just as we do Him from time to time. It makes me nervous to even think about how it would drastically change things. Here is how I think it would play out between us.

Me: Heavenly Father...
God: Hey, Shena, let me get back to you after I check my calendar. I have a lot of important meetings and events to attend. Would you be available at 2:00 p.m.? I could spare about thirty minutes.

I can't imagine how I would feel if this could truly happen. Lucky for us, He is a loving Father, who sees us all as important. With Him, we never have to take a number. He makes sure that He is available twenty-four seven. Sometimes, it blows my mind that He can be with us while also deciding the color in the sky, planting the next lily, and watching over His flock. I can always hear Him saying, "Yes, my child, come."

I felt unworthy writing that, but He quickly intervened to say, "Above all else, I love you." Just as God sacrificed for us, we must be willing to sacrifice for Him. Nothing about what I said is easy. Turning a hobby into a positive habit can be difficult. It can take time, not your definition of timing but God's definition. In our minds, our waiting time would be one year maximum or earlier before we begin questioning if we are cut out for this.

In all actuality, God's timing equates to when He believes you're ready for more. Changing your relationship with God into a habitual one needs to be a gradual process. There is so much to learn along the way. He wants you to get to know Him on a deeper level, for who He really is. But believe me, it will be full of highs and lows. Sometimes, there won't be immediate gratification other than the blessings given to all of us daily—the simple stuff we take for granted, like breathing. The goal of this is to be able to mature in faith.

The more we sow positivity, His love, and His truth into our spirit and into this world, the more unstoppable we will be. Sadness will not be able to hold us down, and feelings of defeat or anger will never prosper. All it takes is for us to glorify our routine. Yes, you read that right. We need to glorify it, sprinkle it, master it, beautify it, and continuously build it up so high that even on a bad day, the devil can't find a peephole.

The enemy will be afraid to even come by your address. He'll probably switch to the other side of the street when he sees you coming because you're a force to be reckoned with. Once you see it, feel it, and believe it, the armor and crown will fit! Take your place to begin your race. One foot in front of the other. One marker at a time. One day, you'll scale mountains and leave your past behind. Let go of that hobby faith. The One pouring has so much more for you.

"Thank you for your patience. Would you like a refill?"

Matthew 6:33

"Seek the Kingdom of God above all else, and live righteously, and he will give you everything you need." (NLT)

Notes

Notes

Prayers

Coffee

AMERICANO	1.25
ESPRESSO	2.50
RISTRETTO	3.10
MOCHA	4.50
LATTE	5.10
VIENNA	6.27
GLACE	7.80
CAPPUCCINO	8.25
MACCHIATO	9.50
CON PANNA	0.95

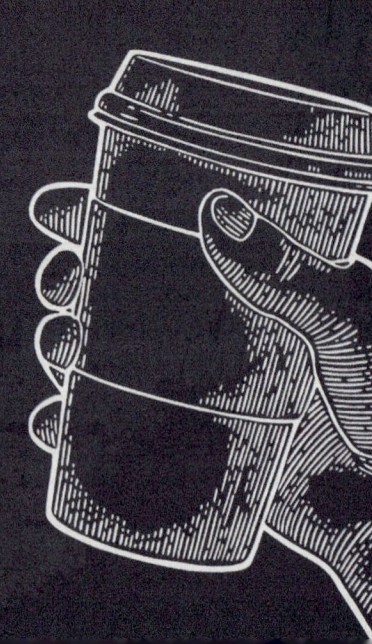

CHAPTER ELEVEN

The Price We Pay

Jehovah Jireh

"That will be $5.75," says the barista. I have been listening to the cash register ring with its familiar cha-ching sound after each sale. What a blessing it is to have such a flow of abundance from something so simple as coffee. It makes me wonder if we all have a price point where we instantly say, "That's all I am willing to pay."

As you know, everything in the world today has a cost. I'm awaiting the day they will say we have to pay to breathe. I am saying that with sarcasm, but you never know what's next. Pandemic-living has truly put a damper on things, and the cost of living is rising. Lord, deliver us from this mayhem. Just joking, give us a little while longer, please.

I've noticed throughout life that I rarely find something of significance that is being given away for free. Actually, I take that back. I do know of one thing I can normally get for free. It comes in different versions, colors, and sizes. I can even draw on the inside if I'd like. Yes, I am talking about the Bible, and yes, if you want the fancy upgrades from paperback, it will cost. But normally, your local church, or our favorite people, whom we try to avoid on the street, will give us one.

You know exactly who I am talking about. The individuals on the street who want to ask you about your faith, then give you a pamphlet and a Bible! I admit it used to annoy me before becoming closer to God. I could never understand why they were always around or on different corners, waiting. I've watched people take the long way around to their desired location or almost dart into traffic to avoid these conversations. It makes me wonder, why is that? Why are we so put off by them questioning our faith? Shouldn't we be able to quickly say, "Oh yes! My Lord and Savior is number one. I speak with Him daily," then take the gifted Bible and go on with our day? It doesn't cost to spare a minute of your day for Him, right? To put it in a better perspective, it cost God His only son to defeat the sin and punishment that was meant for us. It costs us nothing to simply believe.

Yes, I've read how Jesus questioned God about His purpose before bearing the cross. He asked if He must pay the cost, must He do what He was called to do. I can hear it so clearly: "Is there no other way, Father?" I cannot imagine the weight Jesus must have felt at that moment from His human side, but I can tell His spirit knew the victory would be priceless. He knew deep within His heart that He needed to be a willing sacrifice.

Sometimes, I think He could have fought back. He was removing demons, bringing people back to life, turning water into wine, and feeding the five thousand, so was there no way He could avoid paying the ultimate COST for us? He CHOSE to be the payment needed in the transaction of God's Kingdom vs. the enemy, not because it was just another day, but because He loves us and wants us to know God just as He does. He offered Himself to offer us an invitation into Heaven, an invitation into God's personal space, an invitation to destroy the divide and bring us all together.

Thank you, Jesus! How can we ever repay You?!

Lucky for us, He didn't ask to be repaid. He only spoke of continuing His mission—bringing as many people as we can into God's family. The message was clear then, and it is still the same now: share the good news. Our job is to ensure we do our best to continue working towards turning fully to the light. The fee is paid!

God is trying to give us our receipt and ticket into Heaven. It's not an all-expense paid vacation or trip around the world. It's even better! It's a Kingdom pass, a ticket to see Him up close and personal, a ticket to be as He once desired. Are you ready to accept it? Are you okay with the price being free? It costs us nothing to listen, love, and obey. It seems like a small ask or cost when you compare what He endured to what He asks of us. I doubt that we would freely sign up if we were offered to take His place.

Following God won't always be easy. You will be challenged to step outside of your comfort zone, you will have to change some of your habits, and you will be torn about giving Him full control, but if you see it through, you will be filled with renewal, hope, love, guidance, and strength you have never seen before. All I ask is that you spend time in prayer, considering and evaluating the cost of a Christ-centered life vs. one that is not. He is worthy!

"Your coffee has been paid for by the person in front of you. You're all set. Have a wonderful day."

1 Peter 3:18

"For Christ also suffered once for sins, the righteous for the unrighteous, that he might bring us to God." (ESV)

Notes

Prayers

Faith Loading

CHAPTER TWELVE

A Double Shot of Jehovah Shalom Will Do

Parenting with Purpose

"Mommy, can I have the birthday cake pop?" I watch as the mom's face changes to reflect her pondering on filling this child with sugar or battling with the fallout from not giving in. Parenting can be complicated, and when you begin parenting with God's purpose, it can be a roller coaster.

So, I decided to give my life back to Christ and feel like I'm on track most days, but then I realize I am human, and these little people in my house may not have the faith and deliverance that I have yet. How many of us feel like we are tested on a regular basis with our kids? I promise there are plenty of times when I consider taking off my Jesus and asking for forgiveness later. I love the little boogers, but the mouths on these kids nowadays will have you rethinking everything. Where do they get it from? We correct them and teach them respect, but still, it slips right out.

The most famous word in my house is "No" or the tone of telling me rather than asking. Let's not even begin with the "I am playing the game" or "I am busy right now. Ugh!" This is all coming from my eight-year-old. When I had my oldest child, I had no idea he would end up this way, but you know what I had to realize quickly? They are not me. So, let's pray for my youngest now. Hopefully, he will see things differently.

I was raised in a household with limited video game time. Where I grew up, we played outside, we didn't have cell phones, we had some TV stations as long as the antenna hit the right wave, and we knew when our grandma, mom, dad, or the adult supervising us said to do something, we did it. I don't want to say that our children are spoiled, but I do want to say they are different.

I have found myself comparing my son to the younger version of me and sometimes the adult version, putting these high expectations on him of what I think he should be or what he needs to be to get ahead in life. I have learned the more I say it, the more he rebels. Interesting situation, right?

I think, in parenting, we must grow and transition as our children do but understand that they are also born with a broken, sinful spirit. It is our job to show them the light and why it is better to be good. It is never too early to share Jesus with them, begin praying for them, or show them the power of praying themselves. I know it sounds like I am losing my mind, and you're probably wondering, why not whip out the ruler, the belt, or send him for a switch? Not the Nintendo Switch either. I am talking about the branch from the tree that everyone dreaded going to get. I've had my moments, and let's just say it does nothing for my spirit or the atmosphere in my home.

I noticed the toll it was taking on me and my relationship with my son. It was always weighing heavy and distracting me from the time I wanted to spend in God's presence. Anger has always been a downfall of mine. Some people are going to be shocked by that, and others are going to say, yes, I agree. I have always been quick-tempered. My friends used to laugh and call me 0.2 Seconds because that was all it would take for me to become the best version of girl Hulk. I have calmed down a bit as I have gotten older, but I still carry fire around the edge and sometimes a sting to my words.

I don't want my kids growing up thinking that is all Mama is known for. If I do yell at my son, I try to talk to him about how his actions can sometimes determine my actions, and I explain that I need him to understand how respect works. I have also begun seeing this as what I can control and what is out of my control. I can't always control his thoughts or actions, but what I can control are my reactions and boundaries. When he gets out of line now, I immediately tell him he can huff or puff, but we are still going to do what I ask. If he gets too crazy, I ask him to sit in his room until he is ready because we need a break.

I am sharing this because I realize my children are also at war. They don't know as much as we know, but I do my best to pray for them and intercede on their behalf. For the big things I feel like I can't handle, I ask God if I can lay them at His feet.

Now, I am not saying that he is always a handful. There are moments that the little sour patch kid has his sweet moments. I can tell you, though, that this new method is working for our house because he has started to show more affection and emotion towards us in certain situations. That is big for us. We have always thought something was holding him back, but we could never figure out what. We recently got him tested for Autism Spectrum Disorder and ADHD. We were not at all surprised that he had both with a combination of a mood disorder. I have always protected Jaiden from labels or people judging him because he has his quirks, but with him wanting to head back to in-person learning and going into his last single-digit birthday, I figured it was time. I must admit, it felt like a weight was lifted one minute but then heavier than I could imagine the next. We finally have answers and can get him the help he needs to work through all that he feels daily.

I guess what is happening within me and in my home is a shift. He can tell that I am no longer phased as much by his actions. He doesn't carry any weight anymore. You can't argue or be smart with someone who isn't engaging in the same manner. I've learned that my family thrives on my emotions and my energy. If I am having an off day, then they are having an off day. If I don't go anywhere, then they won't do anything. If I don't exercise, then they don't exercise. It sounds crazy, but I'm telling you this because they are watching or listening, even when you don't think so. I have learned to deflect the negative emotions immediately, and you know, the best way I've found to do that is by prayer. I'll start praying out loud, or I'll say, "What would Jesus do?"

I say it so much that Jaiden now feels comfortable enough to say, "Lord, Heavenly Father, hallowed be Thy name, Thy Kingdom come, Thy will be done, on earth as it is in Heaven." For fun, I throw in, "Forgive us, Father. We ask that You come in now to mediate on our behalf. We lay Jaiden at Your feet, asking that You fix his heart, mind, and tongue, so that he is prepared to have a good day." By now, he is just tickled pink that I'm talking to God about him.

He sometimes will ask me if I think that Jesus hears us. These are the moments that I get to disciple him. I call it a "plant the seed moment." Don't ever miss the opportunity to nourish the seeds you have placed. Their curiosity can always lead to something greater. Just for quick reference, let's look at Luke 8:4-15. This passage always gives me hope.

Parable of the Farmer Scattering Seed

"One day Jesus told a story in the form of a parable to a large crowd that had gathered from many towns to hear him: "'A farmer went out to plant his seed. As he scattered it across his field, some seed fell on a footpath, where it was stepped on, and the birds ate it. Other seed fell among rocks. It began to grow, but the plant soon wilted and died for lack of moisture. Other seed fell among thorns that grew up with it and choked out the tender plants. Still other seed fell on fertile soil. This seed grew and produced a crop that was a hundred times as much as had been planted!'

When he had said this, he called out, "'Anyone with ears to hear should listen and understand.'

His disciples asked him what this parable meant. He replied, "'You are permitted to understand the secrets of the Kingdom of God. But I use parables to teach the others so that the Scriptures might be fulfilled:

'When they look, they won't really see.
When they hear, they won't understand.'

"'This is the meaning of the parable: The seed is God's word. The seeds that fell on the footpath represent those who hear the message, only to have the devil come and take it away from their hearts and prevent them from believing and being saved. The seeds on the rocky soil represent those who hear the message and receive it with joy. But since they don't have deep roots, they believe for a while, then they fall away when they face temptation. The seeds that fell among the thorns represent those who hear the message, but all too quickly the message is crowded out by the cares and riches and pleasures of this life. And so they never grow into maturity. And the seeds that fell on the good soil represent honest, good-hearted people who hear God's word, cling to it, and patiently produce a huge harvest.'"

It shocks me every time I think about how God chose me to be a parent, a guardian to His precious children while here on earth. What a big task! Creating and raising a little human is amazing–challenging but amazing. To anyone filling the role of a parent, I am praying for you as well. Thank you for opening your hearts and home. Parenting is parenting, no matter how the family is brought together. All these scenarios call for a bit of wisdom and grace, not just for the children but also ourselves.

- *The pressures of the right or wrong way to do it...*
- *The many "Is it enough?" conversations and thoughts...*
- *The "Did I do enough today?" mindset...*

All we can do is try our best to give our children the right tools to be successful, good-hearted, Christ-loving people—ones who hopefully grow up to be productive citizens who change the world into a better place. A little advice, do your best to be in the moment. If your child asks you to be with them, wants to chat, or wants to show you something, engage with them. If that laundry stays in the basket one more day or those toys lie on the floor another second, so what? No one is coming over tomorrow, and if they are, it better be a good friend, who understands this is a "kids live here" house. Take the time to play outside together. Cut the computer off, put down the phone, and take the tablet; it will be therapeutic for the whole family. Make it fun and plan the day in advance, so everyone is aware of what's happening.

From all of this, I am just asking that you consider picking and choosing your battles. Ask yourself quickly, is it a teaching moment, or is this truly a discipline moment? Does the child need a firm hand or a firm talk? What is driving the child to act out? Game influence, friend influence, medical condition, do your best to pinpoint and change it.

I pray some of what I've said makes sense. I know what I am saying sounds different than what some of us learned growing up, but when you walk in purpose and are looking forward to the day of your divine appointment, something must change. When God opens the book of life and begins to look back, would you be proud of the moments you saw?

"Can we add one birthday cake pop to the order, please? Thank you."

James 1:19

"Understand this, my dear brothers and sisters: You must all be quick to listen, slow to speak, and slow to get angry." (NLT)

Notes

Prayers

CHAPTER THIRTEEN

Room for Cream

The Birth of Reconciliation

Two sugars, two creams, no sugar, no cream, just black, there are too many choices. As for me, I am the kind who fills my cup overflowing with coffee, creamer, and no sugar. Yes, I want all the flavor from the creamer. On those extra tired mornings, I try to opt for more coffee than creamer. As I peer down into my cup filled almost to the top, I think, "Wait, there is just enough space for the cream. I am a professional; I can make it to the table without spilling." And you know what? It never fails that I drop some. The same goes for the coffee shop. I watch them pour, and then oops, it runs over the side. There is something about perfecting the right balance between coffee and cream that reminds me of what my good friend, Jen, told me–to be open to change or healing, you must make room in your heart, just as you make room for cream.

First, I want to focus on the part of the chapter title that states "The Birth." Of course, when we think of birth, we think of the family gathered around and awaiting the newest member. Everyone is smiling and celebrating the joy that is coming into the world. I want to view this from the mother's perspective.

Birth from a woman's perspective is scary, joyful, and, the biggest one, painful. We have been preparing for this day for months. We have been taking amazing pictures and getting tickled by the thought of our baby joining us. As we get closer to the end, we start thinking, where is the finish line?! Even though we know that to get over the finish line, we must endure pain. It is all worth it, but someone should document this pain on a scale of one to one hundred and call it what it is, one hundred!

I give this overview because having to forgive someone and start fresh is like birth. We must push our feelings down, change our mindset, face the issue, and say we are sorry. Opening yourself up to that type of vulnerability and accepting the person again, or trying to move on, can be a lot.

Unfortunately, for me, the person that had given me some contractions in life was my mom. She and I both had strong personalities. She was a young mother, and by young, I mean she had me in her last year of high school. So, you can imagine, she never had a chance to live life or grow up in a normal way. Along the way, things happen, and we must make the best of it. She tried her best and was blessed to have my grandmother by her side, who was a wonderful example for me.

My mom has always had a way with words. I can't think of any other way to say it. Depending on the situation, she could build you up or cut you down. She has had some hurt along the way, and it can show itself pretty easily. I know this now because we have talked about all of it, but it was a great deal to live through. She will openly tell you that she isn't proud of some of her moments when she looks back. I get it; no one is perfect.

When I was growing up, my mom had it in her mind that we would be best friends and do everything together, including going to the club. Yes, the person writing this book and inspiring you at one point went to a dance club, had a drink, and you know what, lesson learned. I dropped that as soon as I hit twenty-one. I had my eyes set on climbing the corporate ladder, and those things did not equate to success.

Since she believed that we needed to be so close, it was hard to pull away from her without her getting offended. I wanted to go out of state to college, no. I wanted to move out into my first home, and she would say that didn't make sense. She didn't like change, and when my now-husband came around, he brought a lot of it. I was leaving on the weekends, or he would be there with me. My best friend and sister lived with us, and she had her own thing going on. There were a lot of moving parts under one roof. By His grace, we made it through.

Let me just say, being an only child did not help. I think she felt like something would happen if I decided to do stuff on my own, like she would be forgotten or left behind. I think she didn't know how to process those emotions, and so she lashed out with her words.

It wasn't until I was about to give birth that I decided maybe I should try my hand at reconciliation and forgiveness. I'll admit, I wasn't the one who prompted the thought. My husband actually came to me after my mom left our home one night, while I was relaxing in my favorite jacuzzi tub, and said, "Shena, don't you think it is time for y'all to talk and get things straight before the baby gets here?" At first, I told him no. I had it in my mind that my child didn't need to be in her life. I didn't want her tainting him, and if she couldn't respect my husband and our home, then we would never speak. As I write that now, I feel convicted by it. I can't believe we went through all of this, but every family has its problems.

I used to speak with my grandmother about it a lot. She was so easy to talk to and always had the best advice. Plus, I never wanted to let her down. She would always say, "Y'all girls need to get along. You're family, and family sticks together." I respected her, so I did think about it. I mean, for goodness' sake, she didn't even want me calling her mom at one point, especially in public. Sometimes, she would ask me to tell people we were sisters, especially if my grandmother was with us. I don't know what good that did, but it made her feel good. Her image and being young were very important to her.

My mom and I had gone without speaking for a while. I had had enough of the back and forth and letting her disturb my vibe and disrespect us. On her last visit to our house, she did something that shocked us all. She put the ball in my court. She explained to my husband and I that she was sorry and had been wrong. She could see that we were happy and building a nice life together. Plus, she wanted to be in her grandson's life. I shake my head now, but she knew that I was stubborn, and when I said I was not doing something or cutting someone off, I would during that time.

I did eventually agree to begin forgiving in baby steps. I started by allowing her to come over more and inviting her to things. We would text or sometimes call. The ball was rolling in the right direction, and I thought, "Great, now this can all be over with."

Fast forward to now, I've been saved by grace, she has grown into her own, and we've made it through the birthing period. Are there days where she says things, and I still get annoyed? Of course. Does she know what she is saying is a trigger for me? Probably not. We are a moving work-in-progress, but we are nowhere near where we used to be. We can sometimes spend hours talking or just work on the phone together. She loves to video chat with her grandkids. I can't take that away from her. She is rocking the grandma role. Well, they call her Ha Ha, and she goes with it. They love her, and it is heartwarming to see them get the side of her that I had wished for all along. I know God has a purpose for her life, and I will continue to pray for our hearts, minds, and reconciliation, especially with it being the two of us now. Sometimes, some of the hardest battles we face are with the closest people we know. My parents and I have come a long way. I didn't speak much about my father in this chapter since I gave backstory about him earlier in the book, but we were also working through reconciliation during this time.

Forgiveness is not easy. Family is not easy. Family members aren't going to be the only ones who hurt you, but when they do, it hurts the most. That's why it is up to us to say, enough is enough. We have one life to live, and when family members are gone, do we really want to leave the relationship broken and experience the should have, would have, and could have thoughts? I don't like regrets. They feel like bigger contractions that are being monitored and will eventually become more painful as time goes on.

Nip it in the bud. Give the flowers now while they are still here, and don't try to rebuild the old but begin with something new. Ask God to purify your heart. Ask God for the right words to express what you are feeling. Begin with a simple hello, and let the Spirit do the rest. No one said you have to love them wholeheartedly right away, but what I am saying is break that stronghold and release that stress. Lay the burden down and move forward. This weight is not something we should carry on our own and throughout life. It will poison every area of your life. Fix it for you. Fix it for your family. Fix it for your place in Heaven. Fix it for peace. Fix it for joy. Even if it isn't accepted, you tried, and trying is good enough. The seed is planted; now, let God work.

Matthew 6:14

"For if you forgive other people when they sin against you, your heavenly Father will also forgive you." (NIV)

Colossians 3:13

"Bear with each other and forgive one another if any of you has a grievance against someone. Forgive as the Lord forgave you." (NIV)

Notes

Prayers

CHAPTER FOURTEEN

Spilled Beans

Honest Expectations

"Not today!" says the barista as the bag of coffee beans hits the floor. I could tell by the tone in his voice that he was not having the best morning. We never really expect to wake up to a bad day or have things go the opposite of how we see them in our minds, but hey, that is life. I know all too well about having honest expectations stirred with faith that spilled out in front of me. My first thought is, "Now I must clean up this mess."

Just like spilling beans, this section is quite hard for me as a writer. I remember trying to write it months ago but couldn't because it felt forced. It felt like I hit a roadblock or writer's block, so I thought. Then one day, after one of the most signifiant, hurtful events of the year happened, the words appeared. I knew then that God had purposely delayed this chapter because I had not experienced what it meant to have honest expectations of Him and then see it not go as expected. What a powerful expression of faith He had set before me. Here is how it started.

When 2021 arrived, I said, "Thank you, Lord. Our family has made it another year." We had been blessed enough not to fall ill from COVID. We were especially grateful since my grandmother was so vulnerable. Our family and her care team made sure to take all precautions before getting close to her. We did everything in our power to ensure she made it through this season.

As the year went on and the vaccine was released, we discussed getting the shot as a family and decided that it was necessary so we could visit each other. We were growing tired of the virtual birthday celebrations and weekly video calls, and let's not even discuss the virtual holidays. It was fun, but not as fun as being with each other. Plus, I had just given birth to a sweet little guy that I needed them to meet. Time was passing so fast, and his first birthday was approaching quickly.

My mom and I had been speaking about celebrating Jax's first birthday and Jaiden's eighth birthday in Virginia. We went back and forth on the dates, but my mom said, "Why don't we plan for the Fourth of July weekend?" I felt like we should have planned for June, but once my mom has something in her mind, it is hard to change it. So, I booked our flight for the Fourth of July weekend ASAP since I knew how busy it could get. I had been telling my grandmother via video that I was coming to see her. She would always say, "Oh yeah?! When?!" With her being eighty-four, we had to repeat things a few times. I laugh at that now, but sometimes, it was hard seeing her like that since I knew her in her prime before dementia set in.

As we were getting prepared to go on our trip, counting down the days, minutes, and hours until we could be together, I received a call from my mom that my grandmother had to be sent to the hospital because they feared she might be septic from an infection in her leg. The date was June 29, 2021. I'll never forget saying, "No, you've got to be kidding, not right now." We were just days away from arriving, and I didn't want our reunion to be in the hospital. No one wants that, right?

Days went by, and it was almost the weekend we were supposed to arrive. My mom called to explain to me that my grandmother was septic and not doing well. Now, you could imagine my shocked response, as we were all just chatting about being together. I fell to my knees and began to weep and pray. At that moment, I heard the words, "Lazarus, LAZARUS." I almost stopped crying because it was screaming so loudly in the middle of my thoughts. I felt confused and heartbroken. I missed half of what my mom was saying because the voice had stepped in.

Her care worker sent me a video of her in the hospital. She seemed weak but knew her name and birthdate. It gave me enough hope at that moment and was just what I needed to lift my spirits.

We arrived in Virginia late in the evening on the Fourth of July. My mom asked if I wanted to go straight to the hospital, but I opted to wait until the next day. In the morning, we all decided to head to the hospital, and when I walked in, my heart sank a bit. I had never seen my grandmother look frail or her age. She was always vibrant and youthful. We had to call her name a few times for her to realize we were there, but when she heard my voice, she smiled. I told her how much I loved her and joked that she always knew if she said the word, I would come running. I'd move mountains if she asked me to. Everyone knows of our love and relationship. Some would call me her pride and joy. She raised me, she pushed me to do great things, and she always wanted me to rise above what was expected but keep my eyes on Jesus.

Each day, I would visit the hospital and sit by her side. We had our moments of sorrow and our moments of joy. I was so hopeful that God heard our prayers and that He would bring her through, as He always has. He was going to show His glory at this moment. Lazarus had to be her.

I went back home on July 12, 2021, as planned since the doctors had told us she was improving. My husband had asked me to stay there with her, but we had two children and school to prepare for, so I thought it would be better if I returned to Florida. Little did I know, by the end of that week, my mom would be asking me to come back. I couldn't believe what she was saying to me: "Your grandmother has to have surgery to help with her wounds. They are saying she may not come out of it. They may need to put her on the ventilator." Whose grandmother are we talking about here?! I knew it couldn't have been mine. I PRAYED and just knew this couldn't be happening. I raced back to Virginia to be with my family.

There we were, in the middle of what was supposed to be a beautiful summer reunion together. But now, on the one hand, we were keeping the kids busy with activities, and on the other hand, debating if we were about to lose the most important person in our lives. What a rock and a hard place we were in, stuck somewhere in the tension between happiness and grief.

I continued to sit by her bed daily and pray. I couldn't let my faith waver; she needed me now more than ever. I almost felt like it was a rite of passage to be there. She was always in my corner when I needed her, and now God was giving me the strength to do the same for her. I felt like ushering in His presence every day was bringing her so much peace. I kept telling myself, "Wow, I would have never been able to do this four years ago. I would have never understood the grace space that we were in as I do now."

I remember the day I called upon my sister, my best friend, to come into the room to pray and worship. We prayed. We laid hands. We knelt before God to ask for healing, the healing that we knew ONLY He was capable of. We believed. We spoke it into existence. We had FAITH. I knew we were shifting the atmosphere and doing our best to bring Heaven to earth because Lord knows she deserved it. My grandmother had not moved her arms since I had been there. She had only moved her head back and forth to look at us, or to acknowledge our questions. The day we brought the anointing oil, praised, worshiped, cried, prayed, and spoke in our Heavenly language, she raised her arm up a little, shook her hand in praise, and smiled. Again, HOPE filled the room. I spoke to God in confidence and said, "Show them who You are, Father. Show them who You are." This was the moment when

I knew He could do exceedingly more than the doctors could. I just knew it.

As the days rolled on, the hospital began telling us that there was nothing else they could do for her. No one likes to hear those words, but for me, I knew I had the ace in this game. I had God working in my favor. My grandmother had COPD and wore a breathing mask, normally only at night. Since she caught pneumonia in the hospital, she was now wearing it twenty-four seven. CPAP is a high-pressure breathing machine, and she hated the thing. I can understand why because it strapped around her forehead and chin and then pushed air into her body at high levels. It helped her but was very uncomfortable. I hated seeing it on her each day. You could tell she was agitated by it, but even with the mask on, I could see her beauty. My nanny was fighting, and I wasn't giving up just yet.

Towards the end of July, the hospital decided that we should begin speaking to hospice. Even in this, I had hope. Everyone else was giving up and wanting me to face the facts, but the facts on my side added up to a Savior who is mighty and full of blessings. Each day, I went to be with my grandmother, we watched TV, I prayed, cleaned her face, or moisturized her skin as needed. Before I left, I would always say to her, "I love you, and no matter what, keep your eyes on Jesus."

Walking through this valley in faith and knowing I was totally out of control, took everything out of me. I didn't want to hear about hospice. I wanted to hear about Lazarus being raised and called forth. I wanted to see miracles, signs, and wonders. I wanted her home where she should be, in her bed laughing at all of us, eating her favorite meals, dancing, working on her word search, asking me what I am up to now, squeezing her great-grandchildren, making memories, and having her cup of coffee. I would have given anything.

The hospital had explained that we needed to decide on whether we would like to take her to a long-term care facility, which would require amputating the infected leg, inserting a trach and feeding tube, wearing the pulmonary mask twenty-four hours a day, and being unable to speak again. Our second option was to take her off the mask to see if she could breathe on her own. We deliberated as a family and thought how selfish it would be to have her here but not as we'd known her. I kept that Lazarus word close in my mind. I thought of how Jesus showed up when everyone else had thought it was too late. I knew even though it looked bad, really bad, nothing was too great for our God.

We decided to opt for mask removal. At that moment, we all felt peace. She was breathing on her own with just a little oxygen. This looked like the blessing that I was hoping for! She opened her eyes, smiled, and began primping her face, as she normally does. It also looked like she had so much to say, but of course, no words came out. She looked just as beautiful that day as she always had to me. I was so grateful for each moment we spent together.

Days went by, and each time I visited the hospital, I remained consistent in my prayer and time with her. The last evening I was there, she was breathing differently and moaning. I asked if she was okay, and her nurses stated they would check her medicines to ensure she was feeling relaxed. We were informed that if she looked strong enough, they would move her to the hospice floor. The funny thing is, by the next morning, they did move her. Hope swooped in again as expected. I wanted to yell, "Celebration time, come on!"

After the move, in the morning hours of August 2, 2021, I was awakened by my mom standing over me. "Your Nanny is gone." Mic drop, heart drop, hope drop, faith shaken, disbelief enters, and now what do we do? If Lazarus wasn't her, then who was the Lazarus for?

My grandmother's celebration of life was held on August 14, 2021. Nothing can really prepare you for picking out a casket, her last outfit, her last jewelry, her last everything. My nanny once told me what she expected if she passed away. "Don't forget that I want pink and white everywhere. My outfit must be this color," she said as she pointed to the magenta pink polish that she made me give her that I just purchased. Her wish was my command. I searched high and low until I found the right outfit and the perfect accessories to match. I will never forget the moment I saw it, a magenta pink skirt suit with ruffles down the front. I knew it was just what she wanted. I cried in the store after clipping on the golden diamond brooch with a white pearl at the center placed on the left side of her jacket, just like she liked it. It was the one; I felt it all over. Her service was everything she could have ever wanted. It was the final curtain call, the day I dreaded forever–life as I knew it had imploded. My heart was broken, and it definitely did not seem like it would be repaired any time soon.

Unfortunately, for me, life still had to go on. Almost two weeks after laying my grandmother to rest, my family was looking at me because it was time to celebrate my birthday. August 25th was always big for me until the loss of my first son in 2011 because our last sonogram was on my birthday. So, every year, my birthday was equated to the beginning of his loss. Now, August had a whole new meaning. I was just beginning to heal and celebrate again when boom, this happened. I joked about why my grandmother couldn't have chosen any other month. I mean, there are eleven others that were available that had nothing to do with me, but would it matter the month? Probably not. I would still be devastated.

I stayed with my mom until September 5, 2021. My husband was kind enough to drive back to Virginia to pick us up. I had kept the children so that he could go back to work. Plus, Jaiden had begun online school.

I dreaded leaving my mom, as this would be the first reality check that she was now alone. When she turned around to head back into the house after saying goodbye, there was no bed there for my grandmother and no noise from the kids. It was just a house, a house full of memories and loneliness wrapped all into one. What a burden to bear. I prayed over this situation and wept, but I knew we could do it.

We arrived in Florida safely. This ride included a very special passenger, my grandmother, who had been cremated. My mom thought it would be best that she came with me since she always wanted to visit me but couldn't because of her health. I cried all the way from the truck to the house and stood inside crying. It was rough. I was handling this situation just how I knew I would, not very well at all.

As soon as I arrived home, my church looked to me for guidance and help to serve. I was mentally and emotionally unprepared, but God's mission doesn't wait. I had continued my Worship Wednesday series while out of town, but there were other items to be handled. That weekend, I went back into serving and making training videos like normal, but on the inside, I was broken. My church family prayed over me and couldn't believe that I was there serving, but honestly, there was no other place I should have been than praising God and feeling His presence. The kids told me how much they missed me, and it helped. I value my position within the church, and I'm grateful for all that our church has done in my life and my family's life.

I felt like I was in the right place and on the road to trying to understand this new life without our shining light. But, little did I know, things were not finished going out of control just yet.

It was now September 22, 2021, my son Dezmond's first birthday. I was about to order some cake or donuts and plan dinner when I began receiving multiple calls from my husband. He was at a job and had become ill. I didn't have the car, as we are a one-car family, and I work remotely now. As he tried to tell me where he was, he began vomiting a lot. I thought it may have been heat exhaustion or that his blood glucose had dropped since he was eating less due to a health challenge he had joined. As I spoke to the woman, who owned the home where he was working, he fainted. I called a Lyft to pick us up and take us to my vehicle. The homeowner called me again to say, "I am calling the ambulance. He sat up from the ground, and his face is dropping." I thought, "This cannot be happening. My husband is having a stroke." I swear, it was like I was having an out-of-body experience. Could I really be at a place in my life where I'd lose my grandmother and husband at the same time? I guess we were about to find out.

I beat the ambulance to the location. He was talking out of his mind, apologizing, crying, and trying to pray but couldn't. His left side was numb at this point. He was panicking, and all I could do was tell him to breathe. I began praying out loud for him. I used the same words I did with Nanny: "Keep your eyes on Jesus. He is here." I also reminded him that he had two boys in the truck, who needed him, so he had to calm down. The ambulance team explained it was just heat stroke, and his vitals checked out. Right then, he fainted again. The ambulance worker didn't believe me and called his name: "Jayshawn, you're good, right?" The ambulance worker hit my husband's arm, and his head slumped over. I knew he was gone at this point. They rubbed his chest and kept calling his name to see if he would come to. Finally, he jumped up like something had scared him.

We got him to the hospital, and it was confirmed he did have a stroke—thirty-five years old, with a stroke. Did you miss that this occurred right after I got home from laying my grandmother to rest and on my first son's birthday, who is no longer with us? At this point, I knew for sure I was in the valley, but why? Why right now? Why this timing? I was in the middle of grieving for my grandmother and son, and then I was almost grieving my husband as well. What was I missing? Was there a lesson in all of this? Was God preparing me for something? Was this a reality check for our family? My husband? All these questions ran through my mind. I was faithful, I served, and I chose Jesus as my one and only Savior; I felt like I was doing everything right, but suddenly, everything was falling apart.

After challenging God for many days, He finally answered, "GET UP! What you do while you wait is important. A warrior is down, but remember your armor. Your flesh is weak, but your spirit is strong. Rise up! Remember what you've always said, 'I lead not with my human feelings but with my spirit.' My work must continue. I am calling you into the deep. I still need you to take your rightful place. You cannot die to the pain. You feel me, and you see me. Come! It is okay to be sad, but you must never give up. Finish what you've started. There is more to come. Nations need you. Heaven needs you. Step into this next season with grace, humility, and the heart to learn. Be ready to encourage others. No more shadows. You are who I say you are, even more now than you'll ever know. Be who I have called you to be. The unimaginable can happen and will happen. Honor me. Lead with understanding."

I woke up the next day renewed. I felt guilty for not crying, but I felt joy that my Heavenly Father had answered through the Spirit. This is the tension that I have been living in now—faith that brings joy and grief that brings sadness.

So, what have we learned:

I had expectations for what God could do.

Was it honest? I thought so.

I honestly thought the oil would work.

I honestly thought the prayers would work.

I honestly thought the worship would work.

I honestly thought...

That year was going to go a lot differently. My flesh wants her here, but my spirit knows she is healed. Grief is hard, especially when you believe in miraculous healing. It's almost like bringing your best weapons to battle and still getting defeated.

But the lesson here is that God's plan is greater.

John 11:4, 41-43

"But when Jesus heard about it he said, 'Lazarus's sickness will not end in death. No, it happened for the glory of God so that the Son of God will receive glory from this.'

So they rolled the stone aside. Then Jesus looked up to heaven and said, 'Father, thank you for hearing me. You always hear me, but I said it out loud for the sake of all these people standing here, so that they will believe you sent me.' Then Jesus shouted, 'Lazarus, come out!'" (NLT)

Notes

Notes

Prayers

- SECTION FOUR -

Until Next time

CHAPTER FIFTEEN

A Full Cup Runneth Over

My Exodus

I've learned so much from writing this book. It has been healing and revealed so much I was still holding onto. This morning, as I was writing and spending time in God's presence, with my favorite cup of coffee, of course, my phone buzzed twice, and I ignored it at first. I didn't want to lose my train of thought, but in my first free moment, I checked my messages. It was two of my close friends, a part of my inner prayer circle, reaching out with songs that God had placed on their hearts to send to me. God amazes me with how He works and communicates just when we need it.

I looked at the song's title, "Freedom Looks Good on You." She had no idea what she had just done for me at that moment. She confirmed that God had heard my thoughts and had seen me work through all of the words and signs He had sent. He had seen my faithfulness and was letting me know that freedom was here. I had finally broken off the last chain and could now freely walk in Him.

As you can see, none of this was immediate. All of it has been a journey. No longer do I need to walk around like I am worried things will suddenly change. No longer do I need to worry if He loves me or if He cares. No longer do I need to hide behind my job title or the number of degrees I have. None of it defines me. God has given me a new name, a new purpose. He has shown me where my life should be focused, and I could never take credit for this elevation, this transformation of not only myself but also my family.

I am so appreciative that God never gave up, and Jesus continued to advocate on my behalf. I am nowhere near perfect, and I still question, "Why me? Is it me? How can it be me?" each time I hear from God, but now I feel like, what can it hurt to express exactly what I need to do? There is no other higher honor than serving Him wholeheartedly and saying, "Here I am." My friends, let's do something crazy for Jesus this year. He gave it all for us. Let's give our all for Him.

Pray dangerously—be specific. Follow in obedience and with a sensitive spirit. Be ready for the highs and the lows. God's way will never be a straight line, and that doesn't mean that He loves you any differently.

I feel something great happening here, but just like that, we are at the end of our time together. I hope God has so much more in store that I can share with all of you as He continues to work on me. The Lord knows I have a mess of emotions, adventures, and unexpected experiences bundled up inside. Hopefully you could tell while reading this book, I was not here to judge but to share how giving God a chance can help you in the great times and the bad times.

He is my strength when I am weak. God is amazing and confusing but loving. A great teacher. He remains on the throne and is the same yesterday, today, and forever.

Maybe the next topic I will approach is changing the mindset. I feel like it has a lot to do with how we see God, but I'll leave it up to the Holy Spirit to guide me.

Words are powerful and transformational, really, and I do not take this lightly.

Philippians 4:4-9

"And now, dear brothers and sisters, one final thing. Fix your thoughts on what is true, and honorable, and right, and pure, and lovely, and admirable. Think about things that are excellent and worthy of praise. Keep putting into practice all you learned and received from me—everything you heard from me and saw me doing. Then the God of peace will be with you." (NLT)

Notes

Prayers

– ACKNOWLEDGMENTS –

THANK YOU....

Thank you to all of the people who are in my closest circle. My mom, my dad, my sister, my prayer warriors, my friends, you have seen my good days and my bad days. You have never said, "You're not good enough," or questioned why I am doing something. You've supported me and respected my walk with Jesus. You know if He calls, I must answer. Thank you for not saying, "She has got to be crazy." Thank you for believing that my spirit is hearing correctly. Having you in my corner goes well beyond words right now.

Thank you to my husband for putting up with me over the years and for listening as I explained to him how we could possibly reconcile. Thank you for taking the chance. Thank you for walking with me along this journey and reminding me to listen to my heart and just do it. Thank you for letting me be me. Thank you for letting me talk your head off about what I feel God is saying next. Thank you for late nights full of laughter and sleeping on the couch. Thank you for letting me birth this new baby into existence. I know it can't be easy letting people see what is behind the curtains, but I know our story will bless people for many years to come.

Thank you to my children for making me feel full each day with love and laughter. You are the greatest gift that

God could ever give. I cannot wait to see the plan God has for you. He has gone before you, and I know that every footstep is blessed, every corner is covered. You are such bright stars.

Thank you to my church family, TNLC, I love you all! Thank you for accepting me in, showing me the way, grooming and guiding me.

TO YOU, THE READER...Let's pray.

Father, I ask that you bless every reader that has taken a moment to step into my coffee talk. My life, my journey, and my testimony all began with You. Allow them to hear the call You have placed on their lives. Break down the barriers that are hindering them. If there is hurt or grief, Lord, I ask that You meet them there. Your peace is the ultimate peace, and if they would just come humbly before You, You would provide them this and so much more. We love You because You are in the fire. We love You because You are our teacher and provider. You are Jireh, You are Yahweh, and You are more than we will ever need. We yearn for the day that we live in Your presence forever but ask that You give us time to build up Your Kingdom here on earth. I hope Your glory can be seen and felt for generations. You deserve it all. Thank you!

Thank you, Jesus, for Your sacrifice and for loving us so purely! Thank you, Holy Spirit, for Your guidance and protection daily!

May we all say, AMEN!

Thank you for allowing me to share with you my personal stories about the war between life and faithfulness.

Philippians 4:4-7

"Always be full of joy in the Lord. I say it again—rejoice! Let everyone see that you are considerate in all you do. Remember, the Lord is coming soon. Don't worry about anything; instead, pray about everything. Tell God what you need and thank Him for all He has done. Then you will experience God's peace, which exceeds anything we can understand. His peace will guard your hearts and minds as you live in Christ Jesus." (NLT)

– ABOUT THE AUTHOR –

Tashena Anderson-Place, the author of *Fill Your Cup*, thrives on being an advocate, innovator, and encourager. She was born and raised in Virginia but currently resides in the sunshine state of Florida.

Tashena was raised in a Christian family but truly found her personal relationship with Jesus in adulthood. During this time, she has been able to grow her faith and learn to fill her cup daily. You can find the author at her home church, serving as the Kids Worship Team Leader, sharing her love of worship and building up the next generation of disciples, planning women's ministry events with some of the most wonderful ladies, praying, donating, or giving back to the community in various ways.

Tashena loves spending time with her husband and children, going on dinner dates with her friends, talking on the phone for hours with her out-of-state family, or you can find her in the kitchen, cooking her latest Pinterest recipe.

Tashena used to be consumed with watching her cup fill with earthly successes such as degrees, certifications, you name it. Now, she hopes to share how pouring out what is comfortable or always your favorite and asking for a refill of the appropriate divine roast that can change your life.

Made in the USA
Monee, IL
19 July 2025

21460711R00105